Live for Jesus

Love, Hope & Encouragement
to Faithfully Follow the Lord

www.GoodNews.love

Live for Jesus: Love, Faith, & Encouragement to Faithfully Follow the Lord

Copyright 2022

Lara Love & Good News Ministry

Good News Ministry

Phone: 843-338-2219

www.GoodNews.love

lara@GoodNews.love

ISBN 978-1-957291-02-4

With all my heart, I ask you to please forgive me! I do my best with scripture(s) references, but am not perfect and also sometimes face technology issues. If there are any mistakes as far as words in italics or bold or verse(s) references or in any other way, I am sorry! Please note I sometimes use brackets […] in verses to add in extra words to help with understanding / application. I encourage you to check verses in your Bible or via an online Bible or via a Bible app on your phone for accuracy and for further study. I read the Bible every day no matter what and live by it as a totally devoted believer in and follower of the Lord Jesus Christ. I encourage you with all my heart to do and be the same!

Dedication

My heart's cry dear Lord

is to live and breathe for you!

To be totally devoted to you

& to help others become and remain the same!

Thank you dear Father

for giving me the gift of writing

& calling me to write devotional messages

& book after book

as part of living for you!

May the messages in this book

bless & encourage countless people

& bring glory to your name! Amen!

A Little Letter from Lara

Dear friend,

I have loved writing since I was a little girl. I love it so much in fact that sometimes I feel like I just can't stop writing! But the one I love more than anything and anyone is the Lord, and I delight beyond measure in loving and serving Him with all my heart and in helping others to do the same.

Never in a million years did I imagine I would write as many books as I have written so far and feel like there are so many more books in me – books for Jesus and for all my precious readers including you. I never dreamed of writing for the Lord! I didn't even believe in Him! Now I LIVE FOR JESUS – and my heart, life, and, yes, my writing, are totally HIS!

May the Lord use this book mightily to help you to have a gloriously intimate, ever-growing personal relationship with the Lord Jesus Christ now & forevermore! May the Lord use it to help you live humbly and wholly, faithfully and passionately for Him! Oh, LIVE FOR JESUS! Forevermore!

I love, love, love to love and encourage and pray for people to believe in and follow the Lord, and you are very welcome to reach out via phone at 843-338-2219 or email at lara@GoodNews.love.

So hoping this book is a big blessing in your life. But as I like to tell people, if you never read a word I have written, that's okay. My heart's desire is that first and foremost you read and live by the Bible. As a totally devoted follower of the Lord Jesus Christ! Hallelujah, LIVE FOR JESUS!

love & blessings, lara

Introduction

Why this book? Because with all my heart I believe the Lord called me to compile 100 devotional messages into another devotional book. Lots of people sign up on my ministry website at www.GoodNews.love to receive the messages I write by email or read them on my website or on Facebook when I post them there, and some read them in my books. What matters to me is not where people find and read them, but that God uses the messages in whatever way He desires with whomever He desires wherever He desires for His purpose – and for HIS GLORY.

Why the title LIVE FOR JESUS? The short answer is I believe the Holy Spirit gave me the title. So I have chosen it in obedience to God. The longer answer is I believe it makes clear a truth it took me a very long time to come to understand and put into practice. A believer in Jesus is not merely to believe. We are to follow the Lord. And we are not merely to follow Him. We are to LIVE FOR HIM. No longer for self, but for God. No longer according to the world's ways but according to God's ways. Not for self glory. But for God's glory.

And in living for Jesus in a crazy ever darkening world where temptations seem endless and so many people are living with their backs turned to God, I believe we need love, encouragement, prayer, help, support, and strength like never before to humbly and wholly, faithfully and fully live for the Lord.

Living for Jesus isn't about a one-time emotional declaration that we are committing our lives to the Lord. It's about every single day choosing to live in loving obedience to God no matter the challenges along the way, no matter the ups and downs, no matter the joys and sorrows, no matter the cost to our flesh.

The messages in this book are filled with love, hope, encouragement, Bible verses, God's truth as far as how to apply the Bible to our everyday lives, and personal testimony.

May you be richly blessed, greatly challenged to grow by the power of the Holy Spirit of God, and deeply encouraged. And may ALL THE GLORY for any way in which you are blessed reading this book go TO THE LORD! Amen!

Special Note

Before you begin reading the devotional portion of *Live for Jesus,* I encourage you with all my heart to please read the VERY IMPORTANT MESSAGE which follows. No matter where you currently stand in relation to the Lord Jesus Christ, there is nothing more important I could ever share with my beloved and precious readers than this VERY IMPORTANT MESSAGE. Please read it! Please hear it! Please heed it! Oh, please do!

The Bible says regarding the Lord Jesus Christ: "Nor is there salvation in any other, for there is no other name under heaven given among men by which we must be saved." Acts 4:12 NKJV

The Bible also says: "Jesus said to him, "I am the way, the truth, and the life. No one comes to the Father except through Me. (John 14:6 NKJV)."

The foundation for life on this earth, for a forever intimate relationship with Jesus Christ as Lord, for eternity with God instead of forever in hell and the lake of fire, for everything good in this life and eternity, for true enduring love, and for this book, *Live for Jesus,* is the Lord and is in the Good News (Gospel) message described simply and clearly in the VERY IMPORTANT MESSAGE I share with you next.

I also encourage you to visit my ministry online, to sign up for my Good News Daily Devotional sent by email, and to read my personal story and a more detailed and deeper telling of the Good News message about the Lord Jesus Christ on my ministry website at www.GoodNews.love.

You are also very welcome to reach out to me at 843-338-2219 or lara@GoodNews.love for help beginning and continuing forward in an everlasting relationship with the Lord!

Very Important Message

The Lord God almighty, Father in heaven, created a perfect world and put people in it so we could have perfect lives and have a perfect forever relationship with Him experiencing and enjoying His love and loving and worshiping and glorifying Him forever and sharing His love with others in perfect relationships with them. But the sins of humanity wrecked this perfect world, wrecked our perfect lives, worst of all wrecked the perfect forever relationship with God we were created to have, and wrecked our perfect relationships with others.

Everything wrong in this world is a result of the sins of human beings. The end result is God's wrath at us for our sins, and the punishment we deserve for our sins is the curse of death, hell, and the lake of fire in forever torment apart from God.

To make a long story short, God the Father loved the world so much He created the one and only way to avoid hell and the lake of fire and to have a relationship with God now and forever in heaven. He sent His only Son Jesus to the earth as God in the flesh to live a perfect sinless life, sent Him to the cross to die to take our sin punishment on Himself, and raised Jesus from the dead. So all who turn from our sins (repent), believe in Jesus Christ as Lord and in His death and resurrection, truly turning our lives over to God and His ways, are forgiven, promised forever life with God, and the Holy Spirit of God comes to live inside us.

God the Father, Jesus the Son, and the Holy Spirit are actually three in one. God in three forms. One true God. The only true God. The Lord!

The Bible says: "For there are three that bear witness in heaven: the Father, the Word, and the Holy Spirit; and these three are one." 1 John 5:7 NKJV

The Bible also says: "And this is eternal life, that they may know You, the only true God, and Jesus Christ whom You have sent." John 17:3 NKJV

Jesus Christ is Lord. He is God. The Bible says:

"And we know that the Son of God has come and has given us an understanding, that we may know Him who is true; and we are in Him who is true, in His Son Jesus Christ. This is the true God and eternal life." 1 John 5:20 NKJV

When we repent and receive Jesus Christ as Lord and turn to the Lord and His ways, we are born again spiritually and begin a lifelong journey of believing in and following Jesus.

What does this life of following Jesus look like? In essence, we are to read the Bible and live by it, be filled with God's Spirit and be led by Him, and live totally devoted to the Lord. Loving Him, praising Him, spending time alone with Him, worshiping Him, reading the Bible, seeking God, praying to Him, waiting on Him, hearing Him, obeying Him, fearing Him, revering Him, adoring Him, serving Him, and bringing Him honor, praise, and glory!

His greatest commands are to love Him with all our hearts AND to love others as ourselves, but this is just the starting place when it comes to others! We are to fellowship with other followers of Jesus as we are all part of the worldwide family of God, God's Kingdom of the children He has adopted when we are spiritually born again into His everlasting family! We are to love one another, share with one another, help one another, encourage one another, pray for one another, support one another in following Jesus, and help bring others into God's Kingdom and help them love and worship and glorify God forever just as we learn to do the same!

For a longer, more detailed explanation and understanding of the Good News (Gospel) message I have just shared with you, and for help following Jesus day by day, please visit my ministry online at www.GoodNews.love where you can read my *Finding the Light* tract which includes my personal story (lara love's True Story) and the Good News message, sign up for my Good News Daily Devotional messages sent by email, learn about my ministry, see my special needs ministry dogs, and more. You can also call me at 843-338-2219 or email me at lara@GoodNews.love.

Please pray to God to lead you to a good Lord Jesus Christ-centered, Holy Spirit-filled-and-led, living-according-to-the-Bible church, Bible study, small group, house church, and/or some assembling/gathering of God's people/followers. That you all may love, encourage, pray for, help, and support one other in being totally devoted followers of the Lord Jesus Christ all the while helping still others to become and remain totally devoted followers of the Lord Jesus Christ! All for the glory of God!

Please find next some wonderful Bible verses to help and encourage you!

"Jesus said to him, "'You shall love the Lord your God with all your heart, with all your soul, and with all your mind.' This is the first and great commandment. And the second is like it: 'You shall love your neighbor as yourself.' On these two commandments hang all the Law and the Prophets." Mt. 32:37-40 NKJV

"As it is written: "There is none righteous, no, not one;" Romans 3:10 NKJV

"For all have sinned and fall short of the glory of God." Romans 3:23 NKJV

"Let no one deceive you with empty words, for because of these things the wrath of God comes upon the sons of disobedience." Eph. 5:6 NKJV

"For the wages of sin *is* death, but the gift of God is eternal life in Christ Jesus our Lord." Romans 6:23 NKJV

"The Son of Man will send out His angels, and they will gather out of His kingdom all things that offend, and those who practice lawlessness, and will cast them into the furnace of fire. There will be wailing and gnashing of teeth. Then the righteous will shine forth as the sun in the kingdom of their Father. He who has ears to hear, let him hear!" Mt. 13:41-43 NKJV

"Jesus answered and said to him, "Most assuredly, I say to you, unless one is born again, he cannot see the kingdom of God." Nicodemus said to Him, "How can a man be born when he is old? Can he enter a second time into his mother's womb and be born?" Jesus answered, "Most assuredly, I say to you, unless one is born of water and the Spirit, he cannot enter the kingdom of God. That which is born of the flesh is flesh, and that which is born of the Spirit is spirit." John 3:3-6 NKJV

"For God so loved the world that He gave His only begotten Son, that whoever believes in Him should not perish but have everlasting life." John 3:16 NKJV

"that if you confess with your mouth the Lord Jesus and believe in your heart that God has raised Him from the dead, you will be saved." Rom. 10:9 NKJV

"Then Peter said to them, "Repent, and let every one of you be baptized in the name of Jesus Christ for the remission of sins; and you shall receive the gift of the Holy Spirit." Acts 2:38 NKJV

""If you love Me, keep My commandments. And I will pray the Father, and He will give you another Helper, that He may abide with you forever—

the Spirit of truth, whom the world cannot receive, because it neither sees Him nor knows Him; but you know Him, for He dwells with you and will be in you. I will not leave you orphans; I will come to you." John 14:15-18 NKJV

"that we who first trusted in Christ should be to the praise of His glory. In Him you also *trusted*, after you heard the word of truth, the gospel of your salvation; in whom also, having believed, you were sealed with the Holy Spirit of promise, who is the guarantee of our inheritance until the redemption of the purchased possession, to the praise of His glory." Eph. 1:12-14 NKJV

"If you then, being evil, know how to give good gifts to your children, how much more will your heavenly Father give the Holy Spirit to those who ask Him!"" Luke 11:13 NKJV

"For as many as are led by the Spirit of God, these are sons of God." Romans 8:14 NKJV

"Then Jesus said to His disciples, "If anyone desires to come after Me, let him deny himself, and take up his cross, and follow Me." Matthew 16:24

"And do not be conformed to this world, but be transformed by the renewing of your mind, that you may prove what *is* that good and acceptable and perfect will of God." Romans 12:2 NKJV

"He has delivered us from the power of darkness and conveyed us into the kingdom of the Son of His love," Colossians 1:13 NKJV

"Then Jesus spoke to them again, saying, "I am the light of the world. He who follows Me shall not walk in darkness, but have the light of life."" John 8:12 NKJV

"So then faith *comes* by hearing, and hearing by the word of God." Romans 10:17 NKJV

"My sheep hear My voice, and I know them, and they follow Me." John 10:27 NKJV

""Not everyone who says to Me, 'Lord, Lord,' shall enter the kingdom of heaven, but he who does the will of My Father in heaven. Many will say to Me in that day, 'Lord, Lord, have we not prophesied in Your name, cast out demons in Your name, and done many wonders in Your name?' And then I will declare to them, 'I never knew you; depart from Me, you who practice lawlessness!'" Mt. 7:21-23 NKJV

""But why do you call Me 'Lord, Lord,' and not do the things which I say?" Luke 6:46 NKJV

"Grace to you and peace from God our Father and the Lord Jesus Christ. We are bound to thank God always for you, brethren, as it is fitting, because your faith grows exceedingly, and the love of every one of you all abounds toward each other, so that we ourselves boast of you among the churches of God for your patience and faith in all your persecutions and tribulations that you endure, which is manifest evidence of the righteous judgment of God, that you may be counted worthy of the kingdom of God, for which you also suffer; since it is a righteous thing with God to repay with tribulation those who trouble you, and to give you who are troubled rest with us when the Lord Jesus is revealed from heaven with His mighty angels, in flaming fire taking vengeance on those who do not know God, and on those who do not obey the gospel of our Lord Jesus Christ. These shall be punished with everlasting destruction from the presence of the Lord and from the glory of His power, when He comes, in that Day, to be glorified in His saints and to be admired among all those who believe, because our testimony among you was believed. Therefore we also pray always for you that our God would count you worthy of this calling, and fulfill all the good pleasure of His goodness and the work of faith with power, that the name of our Lord Jesus Christ may be glorified in you, and you in Him, according to the grace of our God and the Lord Jesus Christ." 2 Thess. 1:2-12 NKJV

"And Jesus answered and said to them: "Take heed that no one deceives you. For many will come in My name, saying, 'I am the Christ,' and will deceive many. And you will hear of wars and rumors of wars. See that you are not troubled; for all these things must come to pass, but the end is not yet. For nation will rise against nation, and kingdom against kingdom. And there will be famines, pestilences, and earthquakes in various places. All these are the beginning of sorrows. Then they will deliver you up to tribulation and kill you, and you will be hated by all nations for My name's sake. And then many will be offended, will betray one another, and will hate one another. Then many false prophets will rise up and deceive many. And because lawlessness will abound, the love of many will grow cold. But he who endures to the end shall be saved." Matthew 24:4-13 NKJV

"And this is eternal life, that they may know You, the only true God, and Jesus Christ whom You have sent." John 17:3 NKJV

"and He died for all, that those who live should live no longer for themselves, but for Him who died for them and rose again." 2 Cor. 5:15 NKJV

...

#1

My Green Striped Socks Story

One morning I put on my lime green and white striped socks a friend had given me long ago only to experience a flicker of terrible sadness. See, instead of wearing the socks myself, I had lovingly put them on my paralyzed dog Mr. Simeon's beautiful long legs when we were located in New York City in the winter on my latest location being on the road for Jesus. He was prone to being cold, and I would bundle him up in two winter coats, my scarf wrapped numerous times around his head, and those green and white striped socks to take him outside for his wheelchair rides with paralyzed Miss Mercy in her own winter attire and wheelchair. But Mr. Simeon's life had ended tragically one day with no forewarning in my hotel room in South Carolina, and I have been devastated ever since being that he was one of the greatest blessings God has ever given me.

But rather than get swallowed up in grief as I have often done over the years with numerous losses, I chose to be thankful for the time God gave me with my beloved Mr. Simeon, to move on with my day with love, joy, and thanksgiving, and to place my heart in the hands of the Lord to receive His amazing blessed comfort with which no human comfort can possibly compare. If you've been grieving a loss, I encourage you to turn to the Lord and pour out your heart to Him, place your heart and tears in His everlasting arms and receive His blessed sweet and tender comfort, turn to the Bible and find love, peace, hope, and joy in God's Word, and go forth in your day – and life - choosing love, joy, and thanksgiving!

"Shout joyfully to the LORD, all the earth; Break forth in song, rejoice, and sing praises." Psalms 98:4 NKJV

#2

My Orange Juice Testimony

I'm not a big orange juice drinker, but one day I found myself really craving it. Unfortunately the store I was in had big containers that would not have fit well in my little hotel fridge along with my other food. And I had a concern about the smaller container not to mention the expensive price for so little juice.

Less than 24 hours later I was standing in the hotel staff office waiting for the assistant manager when I saw small bottles of orange juice. Turns out they were part of the hotel's free breakfast though I had never seen them out for the guests before. The assistant manager gladly gave me a couple of bottles.

Why do I tell you this? God's love for His children is evident throughout our entire lives and forever, yet I wonder are our hearts, ears, and eyes open to all the ways in which He expresses His love even in the very smallest of ways right down to the tiniest of details as with the orange juice? Oh, let us never fail to recognize and thank the Lord for His love and to pass it along to others! Hallelujah!

"Many, O LORD my God, *are* Your wonderful works *Which* You have done; And Your thoughts toward us Cannot be recounted to You in order; *If* I would declare and speak *of them,* They are more than can be numbered." Psalms 40:5 NKJV

...

#3

Beautiful Sunshine on My Face!

I was sitting at my computer in my latest hotel room on the road for Jesus when suddenly the sunshine shone unbelievably brightly through the window and landed and remained directly on the left side of my face. I turned toward it for a moment and relished and rejoiced in something I love so much. Sunshine. Warmth. Light. Brightness. I felt so thankful to God. For decades I took my blessings for granted both in the years I didn't believe in God and in the years I believed in Him but was too caught up in focusing on my personal struggles to notice, appreciate, enjoy, and be thankful for my blessings.

I wasn't just thankful that day for the sunshine, but I was extra thankful. See, I had been on the road for Jesus for 4.5 years, and in most of my hotel rooms the windows wouldn't open and I felt it best for safety and security and privacy to keep my blinds shut. In this hotel, on that day, the blinds were open, the window was open, and God's love poured through the window in His blessing to me of sunshine aimed right at my face.

How many blessings do you suppose we miss along the way and neglect to thank the Lord for? Oh, let us strive daily to see, appreciate, acknowledge, enjoy, and thank God for our blessings! Most of all, let us be thankful to God for being the greatest blessing of all!

"The heavens declare the glory of God; And the firmament shows His handiwork." Psalms 19:1 NKJV

...

#4

Stop Feeling Sorry for Yourself

"Stop feeling sorry for yourself," the Holy Spirit spoke to my heart. "Look at all you have I have already provided."

I didn't even see my self-pity until the Lord saw fit to point it out. I repented. Not just for that. But for the fear, doubt, worry, and anxiety.

I had been focusing on what I didn't have instead of being thankful to the Lord for all He has given me all along the way – most importantly Himself and a forever relationship with Him!

Instead of looking to the Lord and His Word and trusting in Him and being joyful and thankful, I was looking at my circumstances and wallowing in a muddy messy morass of ugly sin in my heart. I needed to turn away from self and turn to Jesus.

What about you?

"Let the words of my mouth and the meditation of my heart Be acceptable in Your sight, O LORD, my strength and my Redeemer." Psalms 19:14 NKJV

...

#5

Feeling Scared?

Feeling scared? I am even as I write this. Not just a little scared. Really, really scared. I am prone to fear, worry, anxiety, and unbelief, and if I am not careful and recognize it as sin and get rid of it promptly, I can spiral downhill quickly, very uncomfortably, and worst of all sinfully. Why am I scared? I am tempted to tell you, but I am compelled by God simply to deliver this message about what to do when we're scared.

The most obvious and tempting thing to do when I'm scared is to try to fix all the issues I have, to get all my questions answered, to figure out the future, to get rid of what is making me scared, to basically go to battle with my circumstances and people whose actions might be part of why I am afraid. But though God may in fact lead us to address different issues through prayer and action, most important of all is that we address our fear spiritually.

How so? May we choose moment by moment TO PUT OUR TRUST IN HIM, TO PLACE OUR FAITH IN HIM, TO REPENT OF ANY WRONGDOING INCLUDING WORRYING AND SELF-PITY, TO SPEND TIME IN HIS PRESENCE, TO LOOK TO HIM, TO PRAY TO HIM, TO SEEK HIM, TO READ AND LIVE BY THE BIBLE, TO WAIT ON HIM, TO HEAR HIM, TO OBEY HIM, TO FIND PEACE, HOPE, JOY, AND MOST OF ALL LOVE IN HIM, AND THROUGH IT ALL TO PRAISE AND WORSHIP AND BE THANKFUL AND TO REST IN AND REJOICE IN HIM EVEN AS WE CHOOSE TO CLEAVE TO HIM AND TO HIS WILL AND HIS WAYS, oh hallelujah!

I smile as I finish writing this. My circumstances haven't changed as I wrote this. But I am so thankful for the Lord using this message to remind me of what to do when I'm feeling scared. Hoping this message brings you hope and encouragement even as God has used my writing it to bring hope and encouragement to me!

"Whenever I am afraid, I will trust in You." Psalms 56:3 NKJV

"Trust in the LORD forever, For in YAH, the LORD, *is* everlasting strength." Isaiah 26:4 NKJV

"Be anxious for nothing, but in everything by prayer and supplication, with thanksgiving, let your requests be made known to God; and the peace of God, which surpasses all understanding, will guard your hearts and minds through Christ Jesus." Philippians 4:6-7 NKJV

...

#6

A Lifestyle of Thanksgiving!

"I am so thankful I don't even know what to do," I thought as I sat perched on my hotel room bed in the quiet of the early fall morning. Oh, such an exceedingly far cry from how I used to live. Miserable. Unthankful. Granted I have had seemingly relentless life's challenges of one variety or another, but never is there an excuse to not be thankful to God for God Himself and for His countless blessings.

Know what came to mind just before I got out of my comfy position on the bed and laid aside my mug of yummy daily smoothie to get to the computer and begin writing this message?

This. We are called by God per the Bible to live a lifestyle of thanksgiving. But I am concerned we may restrict thanksgiving to saying a few quick prayers to God of thankfulness, of telling our friends how thankful we are, or of feeling thankful when the church pastor preaches on being thankful.

The reality? We are to BE THANKFUL in our HEARTS, out of our MOUTHS, and in our ACTIONS. Our thoughts, feelings, words, and actions should show forth our thanksgiving to the Lord.

May seem like a tall order, but when we set our hearts and eyes upon the Lord, upon His Word, and upon all the blessings in our lives, the lifestyle of thanksgiving to which we are called should come naturally as a result of His awesomeness and amazingness and goodness and should be visible to all – most of all to the Lord!

"And *whatever* you do in word or deed, *do* all in the name of the Lord Jesus, giving thanks to God the Father through Him." Colossians 3:17 NKJV

"Therefore by Him let us continually offer the sacrifice of praise to God, that is, the fruit of *our* lips, giving thanks to His name." Hebrews 13:15 NKJV

…

#7

My Mom Forgot the Jelly!

My beloved senior Mom did something so beautiful and loving one day. In my 50s, believe it or not, for the first time in my life, I have fallen in love with peanut butter and jelly sandwiches. So one day when I was blessed to be visiting with my Mom whom I don't get to see for long stretches of time due to my life on the road for Jesus, she went into the kitchen, made me two sandwiches, and blessedly brought them to me. Only problem was when I started on the first sandwich, I noticed something was missing. She had forgotten the jelly! We had a wonderful laugh together, and I still like to tease her about the day she made me peanut butter and jelly sandwiches without jelly. It was all happy and joyful, and I was so thankful to my Mom for how she expressed her love to me – jelly or not. But humor aside, there is a serious message in this – about how we react when we don't get what we want, when people make a mistake, when people fall short, when people let us down, when people forget something, etc.

Far too many times in my life, when people have fallen short in one way or another, from the very little things like forgetting jelly to the very big things, I have lacked love, kindness, mercy, forgiveness, grace, humility, and thankfulness. I have sinned in my thoughts, words, and actions in response to them. Pride, arrogance, judgment, hurt I won't let go of, bitterness, impatience, meanness, judgment, condemnation, slander, gossip, vengeance, neglecting or outright refusing to forgive, not taking responsibility for my own sins in the matter, unkindness, lack of love and mercy, etc.

The Bible says we all fall short of God's glory, and we all love imperfectly and live imperfectly. God commands us to love and calls His children to be a people of mercy, grace, forgiveness, kindness, patience, and the like.

Oh, let us love the Lord with all our hearts in obedience to God's greatest command – and let us love each other with the love of Christ, oh yes, hallelujah, Amen!

"As it is written: "THERE IS NONE RIGHTEOUS, NO, NOT ONE;" Romans 3:10 NKJV

"for all have sinned and fall short of the glory of God," Romans 3:23 NKJV

"A new commandment I give to you, that you love one another; as I have loved you, that you also love one another." John 13:34 NKJV

p.s. I'm finishing up a yummy peanut butter and jelly sandwich as I prepare to publish what I just wrote. This one has plenty of jelly, but no sandwich I make could come close to the blessing of my Mom's wonderful love!

…

#8

Please Do Not Resist God!

If you are clear God is calling you to do something, and you are resisting Him, please stop. Humble yourself, submit yourself to the Lord, and lovingly, faithfully, devotedly follow Him.

Turn from your sins, believe in Jesus Christ as Lord and in His death and resurrection, turn to God and His ways, receive God's forgiveness and the promise of forever life with Him and the indwelling of His Holy Spirit. Spend time in His presence, praise Him, worship Him, sing to Him, be transformed by Him, pray to Him, seek Him, read the Bible, wait on Him, hear Him, seek godly counsel if/when/as He leads you. And when you are clear what God is speaking to your heart, when you know what He is calling you to do, please don't hesitate. Please don't resist God. Don't debate. Don't argue. Don't rebel. Don't run the other way. Don't pretend you haven't heard. Surrender yourself to God and obey no matter the cost to your personal dreams, desires, wishes, ways, and wants.

I was struck one day by the simplicity and powerfulness of what happened when Jesus told Matthew to follow Him. No holding back. He didn't resist God, hesitate, debate, argue, question, argue, rebel, run the other way, etc. Matthew just got up and off He went with Jesus.

May the same be said of us.

"As Jesus passed on from there, He saw a man named Matthew sitting at the tax office. And He said to him, "Follow Me." So he arose and followed Him." Matthew 9:9 NKJV

...

#9

What God Wants Most

Sometimes I feel bad and ashamed that unlike lots of other people I have so few Bible verses memorized, that my memory has declined as I age and I can't even remember some I did memorize, that I don't look like a perfect Christian on the outside as some seem to do though I call myself a Jewish follower of Christ anyway, that my once strong attention span has drastically diminished and usually I can't focus on the Bible for more than minutes at a time, that I fall into sin sometimes even when I desperately don't want to and strive not to like when I become impatient or am exhausted and get irritable, etc. and need to repent. One morning God placed this message on my heart.

What does God want most? I can't speak for God, but I have read the Bible long enough to know some of what matters most to God. And it's not how many Bible verses we memorize. It's not how many Bible study groups we attend and how many answers in our Sunday school workbooks we get right or if we have a perfect attention span when we read the Bible or how pretty our dresses and how good looking our pants and shirts are when we go to church.

What matters most? I daresay it's that we turn from our sins, believe in Jesus Christ as Lord and in His death and resurrection, turn to God and His ways, receive His forgiveness and the promise of forever life with Him, have His Holy Spirit come to live inside us, and live utterly for Him going forth! That we love the Lord with all our hearts, that we love others as ourselves, that we put our faith in God day by day, that we spend time in His presence, that we praise, adore, worship, serve, obey, and glorify God, that we are truly sorrowful when we fall short and repent, that in our love for the Lord and for others we tell others about Him, that we are totally devoted to the Lord, that we long to please and honor Him, that we read the Bible and live by it, that we are filled with and led by His Holy Spirit, that we are a strong part of His worldwide Body of followers and fellowship and co-serve with them. Faith in and intimacy with and a humble and loving and forever-long commitment to the Lord and to following Him, that we live for Him not any more for us, this I believe matters most.

Where do you stand with what God wants most? With what matters most to the Lord? Are you a totally devoted follower of the Lord Jesus Christ? Oh, may it be so!

Here are some verses to encourage you, but may it be said the number one place to learn what matters most to the Lord is the Bible. And be sure to spend time alone in His presence ever praying and keeping your heart open to His Holy Spirit who lives in His followers speaking to your heart what He desires of you personally.

"But without faith *it is* impossible to please *Him,* for he who comes to God must believe that He is, and *that* He is a rewarder of those who diligently seek Him." Hebrews 11:6 NKJV

"I love those who love me, And those who seek me diligently will find me." Proverbs 8:17 NKJV

"and He died for all, that those who live should live no longer for themselves, but for Him who died for them and rose again." 2 Corinthians 5:15 NKJV

"And this I pray, that your love may abound still more and more in knowledge and all discernment, that you may approve the things that are excellent, that you may be sincere and without offense till the day of Christ, being filled with the fruits of righteousness which *are* by Jesus Christ, to the glory and praise of God." Philippians 1:9-11 NKJV

...

#10

Quit Gossiping, Start Praying

If you want to hear something tragic about my own life, it's this. It took me absolutely ages to wake up and realize what in my pride I didn't think of as gossip and slander was exactly that. In my arrogance, and in my ignorance concerning what gossip and slander really are, I did an altogether rock solid job for an incredibly long time calling myself a Jesus follower but treating people in my heart and with my mouth – particularly behind their backs – in anything but a Jesus-honoring way. Sin, sin, sin. Not only did I need to repent, but my wake-up call came with a follow-up wake-up call. Yes, two of them! The second? This.

When we repent and stop gossiping and slandering, when we humble ourselves before God and genuinely commit ourselves to learning to love Him with all our hearts and to love others as ourselves, we have an amazing opportunity to start PRAYING FOR THE VERY PEOPLE WE WERE GOSSIPING ABOUT AND SLANDERING. Imagine. Every negative thing we have thought or spoken about regarding someone else can be turned into an opportunity to pray for them regarding their needs, sins, troubles, struggles, their wrongdoing, their right doing, their challenges, sicknesses, bad manners, absolutely whatever the Lord puts on our hearts to pray for them.

I can't speak for you, but I can speak for me. I am bound and determined to work hard on thinking about, speaking about, speaking to, and treating people with the love of Jesus and to stop missing my opportunities to love people, to pray for them, to help them, to support them, to encourage them, to serve them, to share the Gospel with them, to point them to Jesus, to help them with the Bible, and to set an example for them by humbly, faithfully, devotedly loving and following the Lord with all my heart and loving others as myself.

Want to join me in this new mission of mine? Please do! Amen!

"Whoever hides hatred *has* lying lips, And whoever spreads slander *is* a fool." Proverbs 10:18 NKJV

"Whoever secretly slanders his neighbor, Him I will destroy; The one who has a haughty look and a proud heart, Him I will not endure." Psalms 101:5 NKJV

"Humble yourselves in the sight of the Lord, and He will lift you up. Do not speak evil of one another, brethren. He who speaks evil of a brother and judges his brother, speaks evil of the law and judges the law. But if you judge the law, you are not a doer of the law but a judge. There is one Lawgiver, who is able to save and to destroy. Who are you to judge another?" James 4:10-12 NKJV

"Set a guard, O LORD, over my mouth; Keep watch over the door of my lips." Psalms 141:3 NKJV

"Let no corrupt word proceed out of your mouth, but what is good for necessary edification, that it may impart grace to the hearers." Ephesians 4:29 NKJV

"If anyone among you thinks he is religious, and does not bridle his tongue but deceives his own heart, this one's religion *is* useless." James 1:26 NKJV

...

#11

Do YOUR Job Not Someone Else's

If you look closely in the Bible at the people in Jesus' intimate circle of followers, each and every one had a job to do. They each had a calling from God. They each had their own responsibilities. They each were known and are known through the Bible to this very day for the role they were individually called to play. Their roles and responsibilities, their jobs in life so to speak, their life's work. Their life's calling, this was ordained by God. The Bible makes clear God's followers are called the Body of Christ and that each of us is a part of His Body meant to work together as one whole Body. Jesus' Body. This implies we should only do the job assigned to us by God and not someone else's, doesn't it?

Can you imagine if your feet started to work as hands instead? And if your arms tried to take on the job of eyes? And your ankles of wrists instead? What a disaster this would be! Sometimes in our pride, in our worry, in our overexuberance, in our impatience, in our sin, we disregard the calling and will of God and try to take on other people's jobs they have been assigned by God. Not only do we get in the way of other people's callings and assignments and jobs from God. But we are unable to faithfully fulfill our own.

I am the first to admit I have struggled with this for a variety of reasons including I have since I was young had an extreme sense of responsibility for helping a hurting world so I have tended to scurry around trying to help people and situations even when it was not the will of God. Whatever our reasons for neglecting to fulfill God's will for us and instead taking on other people's callings and assignments from God, this is wrong. The right thing to do – always – is to pray, seek God, hear God, obey, and fully follow God. Where do you stand with this? Encouragement for all of us. Let's do our own jobs God gives us. For the glory of God, oh yes!

"For by one Spirit we were all baptized into one body—whether Jews or Greeks, whether slaves or free—and have all been made to drink into one Spirit. For in fact the body is not one member but many. If the foot should say, "Because I am not a hand, I am not of the body," is it therefore not of the body? And if the ear should say, "Because I am not an eye, I am not of the body," is it therefore not of the body? If the whole body *were* an eye, where *would be* the hearing? If the whole *were* hearing, where *would be* the smelling? But now God has set the members, each one of them, in the body just as He pleased. And if they *were* all one member, where *would* the body *be?* But now indeed *there are* many members, yet one body. And the eye cannot say to the hand, "I have no need of you"; nor again the head to the feet, "I have no need of you." No, much rather, those members of the body which seem to be weaker are necessary. And those *members* of the body which we think to be less honorable, on these we bestow greater honor; and our unpresentable *parts* have greater modesty, but our presentable *parts* have no need. But God composed the body, having given greater honor to that *part* which lacks it, that there should be no schism in the body, but *that* the members should have the same care for one another. And if one member suffers, all the members suffer with *it;* or if one member is honored, all the members rejoice with *it.* Now you are the body of Christ, and members individually." 1 Corinthians 12:13-27 NKJV

...

#12

You Are Judging. Do Not. Pray.

Very early morning. I heard the words clear as day. No doubt where they came from. The Holy Spirit was speaking to my heart. Loudly and clearly. With this message I sensed strongly I needed to share with others.

I had been thinking about a very, very, very large group of people. People many of whom the Lord may in fact be pretty upset with. But God's Spirit who lives inside His followers brought strong chastening because once again I was judging the people. And it is not my place, nor our place, to judge and condemn people.

Pride. Arrogance. Judgment. Condemnation. Fear. Worry. Hurt. Bitterness. A whole bunch of sin in my heart. Enough with it all. Once again, it had to go. I needed to repent. But that was not all.

The Lord brought strongly to mind I had the perfect opportunity not just early that morning. But on an ongoing basis. The perfect opportunity to PRAY FOR THEM.

Simple and powerful directive from God.

YOU ARE JUDGING. DO NOT. PRAY.

Is it possible this message is for you, friend?

""Judge not, that you be not judged. For with what judgment you judge, you will be judged; and with the measure you use, it will be measured back to you. And why do you look at the speck in your brother's eye, but do not consider the plank in your own eye? Or how can you say to your brother, 'Let me remove the speck from your eye'; and look, a plank *is* in your own eye? Hypocrite! First remove the plank from your own eye, and then you will see clearly to remove the speck from your brother's eye." Matthew 7:1-5 NKJV

""Judge not, and you shall not be judged. Condemn not, and you shall not be condemned. Forgive, and you will be forgiven." Luke 6:37 NKJV

"But why do you judge your brother? Or why do you show contempt for your brother? For we shall all stand before the judgment seat of Christ. For it is written: "AS I LIVE, SAYS THE LORD, EVERY KNEE SHALL BOW TO ME, AND EVERY TONGUE SHALL CONFESS TO GOD." So then each of us shall give account of himself to God. Therefore let us not judge one another anymore, but rather resolve this, not to put a stumbling block or a cause to fall in our brother's way." Romans 14:10-13 NKJV

"pray without ceasing," 1 Thessalonians 5:17 NKJV

...

#13

A Challenge to the Churches

Some people do great with this. I don't. At all. You know. The sit-stand-sit-stand-sing-sit-stand-pray-make-sure-you-don't-sing-for-more-than-10-minutes-everything-at-Sunday-church-service-has-to-be-pre-planned-and-run-like-clockwork-or-else. I am not here to judge. I believe God sees our hearts. If we're genuinely loving, praising, worshiping Him, etc. "in spirit and in truth", very strict programmed church scheduling or not, I believe God is blessed with sincere love and adoration for and of Him.

But I wonder is it possible God is offended and dishonored and disheartened and perhaps even disgusted by what is going on in so many modern day American churches with the extreme programming, bright lights, smoky stages, video screens, comedy, expensive stage sets, entertainment, in-church gyms, well-rehearsed worship music with the choir facing the congregation rather than everyone looking upward worshiping God, with Christmas decorations when Christmas trees go against God's Word, etc.?

What if all this were stripped away? What would remain? What would He see in our hearts? And hear coming from our mouths? I wonder what it would look like if all the churches all across the land, and world, would lay aside our man-made plans and let the Holy Spirit lead the way. Some churches do this, mind you. And I would imagine the first Christians likely did.

What if we prayed as long as we're led to pray? What if we sang the songs God puts on our hearts unrehearsed not with the congregation facing the choir and vice versa but with all of us looking heavenward and singing with great passion to God? What if we let people give their testimonies when they yearned to tell the congregation what God had done even if the yearning came at the time the third song is normally programmed to be sung? What if instead of bowing our heads and shutting our eyes when the pastor asks if anyone wants to commit his or her life to the Lord we all had our eyes wide open and people started crying out to God with godly sorrow for their sins desperately calling on the Lord to have mercy on them like they did in the times of great revival long ago?

What if the pastors preached the whole Truth of the Bible leaving nothing out even if all the people ran away when the pastor preached on sin, heaven, and hell and called the people to repentance and a life of obedience and holiness? What if the pastors didn't sugar coat God's Truth to please the people and keep the church pews filled?

And what if when it comes to Thanksgiving, whether we're in the church building or out walking our dogs or sitting on our front porches or crying in our jail cells or smooshed up in a tiny bunk bed at our homeless shelters or driving cross country to a funeral service thinking about God we simply and sincerely started calling out to God in our hearts or even boisterously aloud to tell Him how THANKFUL we are?

What if our Thanksgiving alone with God and in the presence of others poured from our hearts, mouths, and lives continually as well it should?

What if we got rid of all our human-made regulations and rules and restrictions and as long as we did things "decently and in order (1 Cor. 14:14)" to honor God we lay all the human traditions and programs and agendas and church comforts aside and simply humbled ourselves before God almighty and loved and praised and thanked and worshiped the Lord with every single ounce of our hearts? And what if we all went all out getting out of the pews and going beyond the church walls to tell the world about the Lord Jesus Christ and how to have forever life with God instead of spend eternity apart from Him in torment in hell and the lake of fire?

May all who read this message and I humble ourselves, cry out to God, and make any and all changes in our hearts and lives so God is loved, honored, praised, obeyed, served, thanked, and glorified by us this very day and forevermore! Glory be to the Lord! Amen!

"But the hour is coming, and now is, when the true worshipers will worship the Father in spirit and truth; for the Father is seeking such to worship Him. God *is* Spirit, and those who worship Him must worship in spirit and truth." John 4:23-24 NKJV

...

#14

I Love Kindness BUT -

"I love kindness," I said aloud after hanging up the phone. I had been speaking with someone at a government office with whom I had spoken before. Helpful. Kind. Such a blessing especially in this day and age. I would suppose most of us appreciate kindness. And I would imagine many of us are thankful for kindness when we receive it. And probably lots of us don't like it when we don't receive kindness. But I wonder this.

Are we more focused on whether or not we receive kindness than we are dedicated to being kind to others?

How quickly and easily I have gotten upset over the years when people have been unkind to me. But how terribly far short I have fallen in showing kindness toward others.

The Lord shows us in the Bible His greatest commands are to love Him with all our hearts and to love others as ourselves, His Holy Spirit lives inside His followers whereby we are to bear the fruit of His Spirit which includes kindness, we are to "put on" kindness, and love is to be kind. There is no way around it. God's followers are to be people of love and kindness.

Are we kind to others? Do we repent before God when we are not? Do we apologize to people when we are unkind? Let's seek the Lord about this. Let's repent if we need to. Let's strive to be kind. Through the love of God, by the love, grace, mercy, strength, and power of the Holy Spirit, through Jesus, let us be kind!

Our kindness should not be contingent on whether or not others are kind. We should humble ourselves before the Lord and in obedience to Him BE KIND! Each and every day, with the love of Jesus, for the glory of God, let us BE KIND!

"Jesus said to him, 'YOU SHALL LOVE THE LORD YOUR GOD WITH ALL YOUR HEART, WITH ALL YOUR SOUL, AND WITH ALL YOUR MIND.' This is *the* first and great commandment. And *the* second *is* like it: 'YOU SHALL LOVE YOUR NEIGHBOR AS YOURSELF.' On these two commandments hang all the Law and the Prophets." Matthew 22:37-40 NKJV

"Love suffers long *and* is kind; love does not envy; love does not parade itself, is not puffed up;" 1 Corinthians 13:4 NKJV

"Therefore, as *the* elect of God, holy and beloved, put on tender mercies, kindness, humility, meekness, longsuffering;" Colossians 3:12 NKJV

"But the fruit of the Spirit is love, joy, peace, longsuffering, kindness, goodness, faithfulness, gentleness, self-control. Against such there is no law." Galatians 5:22-23 NKJV

…

#15

I Was Tempted to QUIT

You might be surprised how many times over the years I have been tempted to quit. To quit life altogether – and to quit ministry. It's been a good long while since I was tempted to quit life, and I give God all the glory for that miracle. But just yesterday I had thoughts about quitting ministry – for the umpteenth time. Perhaps you want to know why, and I can tell you briefly. But this message isn't about why at times I have been tempted to quit. It's about the exact opposite. It's about NOT QUITTING when we're tempted to quit.

The why? Being totally devoted to the Lord Jesus Christ and being in ministry 24-7 with very little help and support in this day and age with all its challenges coupled with my personal struggles combined with how ferociously the devil attacks and tempts me at times adds up to every once in a while being tempted to quit. Enough said.

So let me tell you about NOT quitting with the hope you might be encouraged in your own life when you're tempted to quit something – or someone.

When we're clear God has called us to something or someone, we can CHOOSE TO OBEY GOD. We can CHOOSE NOT TO QUIT. But when we're tempted incredibly hard to quit, even if we don't want to quit, how can we stick with whatever or whomever God has called us to?

When we love the Lord with all our hearts as we are commanded to do and want to please, honor, obey, serve, adore, praise, worship, and glorify God as we should desire to do, THE LORD WILL GIVE US ALL WE

NEED TO NOT QUIT. He will give us EVERYTHING necessary to press on.

No matter how much I've been tempted over the years to quit life or something in my life including ministry, this is what I have done to not fall into the temptation of quitting. I recommend if/as/when the Lord leads you that you do the same!

- Turn to the Lord.
- Cry out to the Lord.
- Seek the Lord.
- Pray to the Lord.
- Pour out my/your heart to the Lord.
- Spend time alone in His presence.
- Read the Bible and live by it.
- Listen for God's voice speaking to my/your heart.
- Humble myself/yourself before Him.
- Make a conscious effort to praise and worship and sing to Him even when I/you struggle.
- Reach out to my/your fellow Jesus followers for love, prayer, encouragement, and support.
- CHOOSE to obey Him.
- CHOOSE to keep going forward IN THE STRENGTH OF GOD FOR THE GLORY OF GOD!

I have written a number of devotional messages over the years about not quitting. And I will likely write more. I believe we could all use encouragement when it comes to refusing to quit when God is leading us to carry on!

"Brethren, I do not count myself to have apprehended; but one thing *I do,* forgetting those things which are behind and reaching forward to those things which are ahead, I press toward the goal for the prize of the upward call of God in Christ Jesus." Philippians 3:13-14 NKJV

...

#16
I Ran Out of Luck!

I would be blown away by how many people say things like, "Good luck!" and "I was lucky" and "I ran out of luck" except for the fact I once fell for this myself. This business of believing in luck and being lucky and wishing other people luck and such. The Lord has since corrected me. Now that I know God is Creator, all powerful, all knowing, Lord of Lords, King of Kings, almighty God, Father in heaven, etc., I don't mess around with using the word LUCK.

 I try to use every opportunity God gives me not to tell people that I am lucky. But to tell people about the Lord Jesus Christ. To give God EVERY SINGLE OUNCE OF GLORY He is due. My life is not filled with luck. My life is filled with the unfathomable love and matchless grace and immeasurable mercy and indescribably wonderful goodness and over-the-top greatness and magnificent majesty and stupendously stunning splendor of God almighty in Christ.

I encourage all whose eyes fall upon this message to reconsider using the words LUCK and LUCKY. Let us give the Lord the glory due His name. He is worthy of ALL praise, honor, and glory forevermore, AMEN!

"saying: "Amen! Blessing and glory and wisdom, Thanksgiving and honor and power and might, *Be* to our God forever and ever. Amen."" Revelation 7:12 NKJV

p.s. Instead of telling people, "Good luck," let us speak words that point people to the Lord!

. . .

#17

Reaching the Unreachable

I wanted to title this message "praying through walls," but the words "reaching the unreachable" poured out instead. It's all the same to me. I have a heart for the people around the world in the most dire straits. "The least of these," per the Bible. So many of them are unreachable for different reasons.

Too far away to help, hearts too hard to listen, too rebellious to hear and turn to the Lord, being persecuted in isolation, seemingly too far gone to have any hope for them, too many of them to reach all of them, speaking languages I don't know, in hospitals and nursing homes and prisons with no or limited visitors allowed, many, many of them neglected, abandoned, overlooked, and forgotten, and this is just the beginning of it all.

Walls, walls, walls, so many walls. Walls of separation and isolation and impossibility to go and help and tell them all about Jesus, talk to them about the Bible, encourage them, love, them, love them, oh, to love them, and help in ways they need help.

But not a single physical, emotional, or spiritual "wall" is too big, strong, powerful, and impossible for God to go through and to reach the unreachable. And there is one way every single human on this earth who believes in and follows the Lord Jesus Christ can help reach the unreachable.

Oh, let us pray! Continually! For every person worldwide the Lord puts on our hearts to pray for. No matter the walls. No matter the seeming impossibility of it all. Let us put our trust in the Lord most high and PRAY! Amen!

Please, from the bottom of my heart, I implore you, don't pray religiously just before a meal and for your family before bed. Don't just pray in church on Sundays or when a friend grabs your hand and says, "Let's pray." Don't just pray when you have an all-out emergency.

May every human on this earth who professes Jesus Christ as Lord pray, pray, and pray on an ongoing basis according to the Lord as He places on our hearts whom to pray for, what to pray for and about, when to pray, oh, to God be the glory, AMEN!

"pray without ceasing," 1 Thessalonians 5:17 NKJV

"These things I have written to you who believe in the name of the Son of God, that you may know that you have eternal life, and that you may *continue to* believe in the name of the Son of God. Now this is the confidence that we have in Him, that if we ask anything according to His will, He hears us. And if we know that He hears us, whatever we ask, we know that we have the petitions that we have asked of Him." 1 John 5:13-15 NKJV

"Then He spoke a parable to them, that men always ought to pray and not lose heart, saying: "There was in a certain city a judge who did not fear God nor regard man. Now there was a widow in that city; and she came to him, saying, 'Get justice for me from my adversary.' And he would not for a while; but afterward he said within himself, 'Though I do not fear God nor regard man, yet because this widow troubles me I will avenge her, lest by her continual coming she weary me.' " Then the Lord said, "Hear what the unjust judge said. And shall God not avenge His own elect who cry out day and night to Him, though He bears long with them? I tell you that He will avenge them speedily. Nevertheless, when the Son of Man comes, will He really find faith on the earth?'"" Luke 18:1-8 NKJV

…

#18

I Veered Way Off Course

Years ago when I was totally broken I cried tons. Now I don't cry so often. I've been really crying hard for the past few minutes. Godly sorrow produces repentance. That's when we're really truly sorry about our sins and how we've disobeyed and hurt and rebelled against God. This is why I'm crying. Because I did something terrible without even seeing it. And God in His amazing love and mercy just led me to repentance. See, I veered way of course.

I had absolutely no intention of sinning. I didn't want to hurt God in the least. I didn't want to hurt anyone. And I didn't want to hurt myself either. But in one big fell swoop I fell big-time into sin and veered way off course. Now this message comes with a warning, friend. See, there was NOTHING about what I did that anyone would think was wrong. In fact, many people knew about what I did. In the grand scheme of things, it seemed right, godly, righteous, good, etc. But herein lies the warning. Sin against God isn't always doing something really bad. Sometimes it's doing something good but that is NOT GOD'S WILL FOR OUR LIVES. It's God's will for other people but not for us.

That's what happened to me. What seemed right to me wasn't right because it wasn't what God wanted for me. So in that sense I veered off course. It was something He has given others to do. And because I jumped right in and got all busy doing it, I was unable to show up for God and His will for me the way I so desperately wanted to do.

Now there is a second warning with this message about veering off course. Even if it had been right for me, God showed me MY HEART WAS WRONG. My motives were wrong. Oh, sure, on the surface I had some good intentions. But deep down inside me, there was sin in my heart. My underlying purposes were wrong. Sin. So I was off course with my actions and with my motives behind them.

I could have gone on for years in this sin. But God in His love for me chastened me, led me to repentance, and forgave me.

How do I feel right now? Drained. Sad. Disappointed. And so very thankful. I asked God why He let me do it. He spoke to my heart that He wanted me to see. I believe He was testing me. And that He wanted me to see what needed to be purged from my heart and life. And where there needs to be way more trust in Him and accompanying growth.

So now I ask you, friend. Is there anywhere in your life in which you have veered off course? Please go before the Lord and see what He shows you and speaks to your heart. And if you needed to do as I have done, i.e. humble yourself and repent, please do. For the glory of God, amen!

"Now I rejoice, not that you were made sorry, but that your sorrow led to repentance. For you were made sorry in a godly manner, that you might suffer loss from us in nothing. For godly sorrow produces repentance *leading* to salvation, not to be regretted; but the sorrow of the world produces death." 2 Corinthians 7:9-10 NKJV

"Have mercy upon me, O God, According to Your lovingkindness; According to the multitude of Your tender mercies, Blot out my transgressions. Wash me thoroughly from my iniquity, And cleanse me from my sin. For I acknowledge my transgressions, And my sin *is* always before me. Against You, You only, have I sinned, And done *this* evil in Your sight—That You may be found just when You speak, *And* blameless when You judge. Behold, I was brought forth in iniquity, And in sin my mother conceived me. Behold, You desire truth in the inward parts, And in the hidden *part* You will make me to know wisdom. Purge me with hyssop, and I shall be clean; Wash me, and I shall be whiter than snow. Make me hear joy and gladness, *That* the bones You have broken may rejoice. Hide Your face from my sins, And blot out all my iniquities. Create in me a clean heart, O God, And renew a steadfast spirit within me. Do not cast me away from Your presence, And do not take Your Holy Spirit from me. Restore to me the joy of Your salvation, And uphold me *by Your* generous Spirit. *Then* I will teach transgressors Your ways, And sinners shall be converted to You. Deliver me from the guilt of bloodshed, O God, The God of my salvation, *And* my tongue shall sing aloud of Your righteousness. O Lord, open my lips, And my mouth shall show forth Your praise. For You do not desire sacrifice, or else I would give *it;* You do not delight in burnt offering. The sacrifices of God *are* a broken spirit, A broken and a contrite heart—These, O God, You will not despise." Psalms 51:1-17 NKJV

…

#19

My Big PURGE PRAYER

Every once in a while over the years I have felt shocked, hurt, horrified, saddened, and sometimes even devastated over losing someone or some people or some thing or many things in my life seemingly all at once. Now sometimes this has had nothing to do with me whatsoever, but other times it absolutely has had to do with me. And here is why. It has to do with my big PURGE PRAYER I have prayed to God a number of times over the course of time.

"Lord, please take every person, place, and thing you want out of my life. And please put in my life every person, place, and thing you want in it." Now sometimes I leave out the part about putting in my life the people, places, and things God desires to put in it. But the PURGE aspect anyway isn't about what God brings into my life. It's about what He has taken out! Let me give you an example.

Just yesterday the Lord took something HUGE that I was REALLY EXCITED about out of my life. Just like that. It seemed to come out of nowhere. I absolutely could not see it coming. Then all of a sudden I remembered that JUST ONE DAY BEFORE I had prayed with a brother in the Lord, "Please God take every person, place, and thing you want out of our lives." Oh my! God had answered my prayer! My big PURGE PRAYER had sounded really humble and noble and honoring to the Lord as I prayed it. But I hadn't imagined how He would answer it!

So here is the thing. And I have shared this in my writing countless times. GOD ALWAYS KNOWS WHAT IS BEST. When we ask God to take out of our lives every person, place, or thing He wants out of our lives, we can rest assured HE WILL ANSWER THIS PRAYER AND ALL OUR PRAYERS ACCORDING TO HIS PERFECT WILL IN HIS PERFECT TIMING FOR HIS ALMIGHTY GLORY AND CONCERNING WHAT IS BEST FOR WE WHO ARE HIS CHILDREN AND SERVANTS!

I won't be surprised if God does more purging in my life in the near future. And I know the very best response I can have to God's answer to my big PURGE PRAYER is to TRUST HIM, TO BE THANKFUL TO HIM, TO REJOICE IN HIM, TO ABIDE IN HIM, TO FOLLOW HIM, and TO GLORIFY HIM!

Led to say the prayer?

As I wrap up this message, these verses come to mind. May they be an encouragement to us all!

""I am the true vine, and My Father is the vinedresser. Every branch in Me that does not bear fruit He takes away; and every *branch* that bears fruit He prunes, that it may bear more fruit. You are already clean because of the word which I have spoken to you. Abide in Me, and I in you. As the branch cannot bear fruit of itself, unless it abides in the vine, neither can you, unless you abide in Me. "I am the vine, you *are* the branches. He who abides in Me, and I in him, bears much fruit; for without Me you can do nothing. If anyone does not abide in Me, he is cast out as a branch and is withered; and they gather them and throw *them* into the fire, and they are burned." John 15:1-6 NKJV

. . .

#20

This is NOT Sexy

When I reflected on the big sin I had fallen into, I realized how "sexy" it had seemed at the time. Now let me be clear. First, my sin had NOTHING to do with men, relationships, sexual relations, etc. The word "sexy" can be defined as "appealing". Second, what I fell into was actually GOOD and GODLY not ungodly and unrighteous. It simply wasn't God's will for MY life even though it seems to be God's will for many other people's lives. Bottom line? The sin was super tempting, appealing, tantalizing, alluring, and exciting. Of course, behind the sin, lurking in the shadows, was Satan dangling the "sexy" sin in front of me. And there is absolutely NOTHING "sexy" about the consequences of sin!

There is all sorts of sin, but there is only one who stands behind it all. Satan who is on an all out mission to steal, kill, and destroy (John 10:10). And no matter how "sexy" he tries to make sin seem, SIN IS WRONG, DANGEROUS, AND DEADLY AND MUST BE GOTTEN RID OF. Sin is awful and terrible and comes with horrible consequences. Sin hurts God, sin hurts others, and sin hurts ourselves. Sin comes with short-term consequences, long-term consequences, and eternal consequences. Nothing "sexy" about any of this!

No matter how "sexy" sin seems, there is only one right way to handle it. In the strength of God, for the glory of God, we need to say NO if we haven't yet fallen into it and repent and turn to the Lord if we already have.

Don't be fooled by sin seeming "sexy", friend. ALL SIN must go! We need to turn away from it ALL! For Christ's sake, AMEN!

"But each one is tempted when he is drawn away by his own desires and enticed. Then, when desire has conceived, it gives birth to sin; and sin, when it is full-grown, brings forth death." James 1:14-15 NKJV

"Be sober, be vigilant; because your adversary the devil walks about like a roaring lion, seeking whom he may devour. Resist him, steadfast in the faith, knowing that the same sufferings are experienced by your brotherhood in the world." 1 Peter 5:8-9 NKJV

…

#21

I Am So Tired of Bad News!

I am so tired of bad news! I can barely keep up with it. It's not always my own bad news. Rest assured I have had decades of seemingly relentless struggles, trials, tragedies, tribulations. But everywhere I turn it seems people have bad news to share.

I don't watch television and only look at the news very briefly online, but people are constantly telling me about bad stuff happening. I know I am not alone in terms of being tired of it all. And I am writing this not to moan and groan about all the bad news and to bring you down, but to share with you the most wonderful good news and hope in the universe and to tell you how I've learned to be up and positive and hopeful and joyful and deeply satisfied even when the world is filled with ever more bad news.

The BEST NEWS IN THE UNIVERSE is that God almighty has provided a way for us to have a personal intimate wonderfully glorious totally fulfilling relationship with Him on this earth and FOREVER IN HEAVEN where there will not be a single ounce of bad news not ever. And the way to be up and positive and hopeful and joyful and deeply satisfied even when the world is filled with ever more bad news is TO FOCUS ON THE LORD AND THE BIBLE AND TO ABIDE IN HIM AND FULFILL HIS WILL FOR OUR LIVES.

In a nutshell, everything bad in this world is a result of sin that separates us from God and means all humans are under the curse for our sins of God's wrath, death, hell, and the lake of fire. But God loved us so much He sent His only Son Jesus to live a perfect life on earth then to die on the cross to pay our sin penalty and to be raised from the dead. So all who turn from our sins, believe in Jesus as Lord and in His death and resurrection, truly turning our lives over to God and His ways, are forgiven, promised forever life with God, and have the Holy Spirit come live inside us.

Friend, NO MATTER HOW MUCH BAD NEWS WE HAVE IN THIS WORLD, we can surrender our lives to the Lord and learn to ABIDE IN HIM. Abide? Trust in Him, rest in Him, rejoice in Him, find comfort in Him, have hope in Him, fellowship with Him, commune with Him, praise and worship Him, serve and adore Him, sing to Him, enjoy His company, find wisdom in Him, glorify Him, have the best friendship ever with Him, find peace in Him, receive and experience His magnificent love, put our expectation in Him, look to Him, pray to Him, seek Him, hear Him, and follow Him.

Even as I write this message, my heart has lifted up. My hope has increased. My joy has surged. And I am so thankful, so very, very thankful, to encourage you to take your eyes off all the bad in this world and set your heart on the Lord and live day and night to love and glorify Him now and forevermore, AMEN! Oh, hallelujah! Not just good news. The best news! The Lord Jesus Christ – forever and ever GOD! Amen!

"You will keep *him* in perfect peace, *Whose* mind *is* stayed *on You,* Because he trusts in You." Isaiah 26:3 NKJV

…

#22

This is Satan Taunting You

This is Satan taunting you. The words came strongly and clearly in my heart as I drove down the highway early one morning. The Holy Spirit was warning me. I was about to take the bait. Satan was coming after me early to wreck my day. The devil loves to aim fiery darts at us, tempt us with anything and everything, attack us from any and all sides, go all out in his mission to steal, kill, and destroy (John 10:10), and on top of it all disguise himself so we don't recognize him and take the bait he dangles tauntingly in front of us.

I was thinking about a whole bunch of stuff and at the cusp of getting pretty riled up and upset. But God in His love and graciousness stepped in to warn me.

By God's grace, I made the right decision. I chose not to fall for the devil's taunts and temptations. Yet I knew the devil wasn't done with me. He would come back with further attempts to wreck my relationship with God and get me off course of life and ministry. I knew what I would need to do each and every time the devil would come my way. The same thing we all need to do. Submit ourselves to God, resist the devil, and draw near ever nearer to God and to His Word. Please keep your eyes, ears, and heart wide open to God warning you when the devil is coming at you, and please surrender all to the Lord and resist Satan in the strength of Christ for the glory of Christ, Hallelujah, AMEN!

Satan can taunt us all he wants, but Jesus' followers can rest assured we can have victory in and through the Lord!

"Be sober, be vigilant; because your adversary the devil walks about like a roaring lion, seeking whom he may devour. Resist him, steadfast in the faith, knowing that the same sufferings are experienced by your brotherhood in the world." 1 Peter 5:8-9 NKJV

"Therefore submit to God. Resist the devil and he will flee from you. Draw near to God and He will draw near to you. Cleanse *your* hands, *you* sinners; and purify *your* hearts, *you* double-minded." James 4:7-8 NKJV

"Finally, my brethren, be strong in the Lord and in the power of His might. Put on the whole armor of God, that you may be able to stand against the wiles of the devil. For we do not wrestle against flesh and blood, but against principalities, against powers, against the rulers of the darkness of this age, against spiritual *hosts* of wickedness in the heavenly *places.* Therefore take up the whole armor of God, that you may be able to withstand in the evil day, and having done all, to stand. Stand therefore, having girded your waist with truth, having put on the breastplate of righteousness, and having shod your feet with the preparation of the gospel of peace; above all, taking the shield of faith with which you will be able to quench all the fiery darts of the wicked one. And take the helmet of salvation, and the sword of the Spirit, which is the word of God; praying always with all prayer and supplication in the Spirit, being watchful to this end with all perseverance and supplication for all the saints— and for me, that utterance may be given to me, that I may open my mouth boldly to make known the mystery of the gospel, for which I am an ambassador in chains; that in it I may speak boldly, as I ought to speak." Ephesians 6:10-20 NKJV

…

#23

Don't Let Your Emotions Stop You!

Maybe you're not a very emotional person. Maybe you are. Some people are. Some aren't. If you know me, you know I am. We all have emotions. Feelings. Think about it. I feel good. I feel bad. I feel tired. I feel sad. I feel happy. I feel strongly about this. I feel afraid. I am worrying. I feel hurt. I feel devastated. I feel excited. I feel elated. I feel like doing something. I absolutely don't feel like doing that. I'm not in the mood. I'm so incredibly angry at them. I feel so bitter. I am so jealous of her. Emotions, emotions. We can be driven by our emotions.

When in fact we're supposed to not live according to our feelings but instead to be led by God. Emotions aren't to rule and reign in our hearts and lives. God is. And sometimes if we're not careful we may allow our emotions to stop us from seeking and fulfilling God's will for us.

Are you allowing your emotions in any way to stop you from fulfilling God's will for you day by day?

Examples. God instructs you to apply for a new job. You allow fear to stop you from applying. God leads you to share the Gospel with your quilting group. You're worried about what they think and refuse to do it. God wants you to pray for three people down the street but you're angry at them and refuse to pray. God is calling you to start a ministry but you're feeling depressed and choose instead to hide under the covers knowing full well God will give you the love, resources, courage, and strength to start the ministry. God commands you to love and forgive but you're holding onto that really old hurt and won't budge whatsoever when it comes to those family members you don't talk to anymore. Get the point? We can allow our feelings to stop us from following God.

If you are allowing your emotions to stop you from fulfilling God's will for your life day by day, it's time to stop. And it's time to start yielding to the rule and reign of God almighty in your life now and forevermore, AMEN!

"I delight to do Your will, O my God, And Your law *is* within my heart."" Psalms 40:8 NKJV

"For as many as are led by the Spirit of God, these are sons of God." Romans 8:14 NKJV

...

#24

Not Your Job – Stay Focused!

"Not your job – stay focused!" the Holy Spirit spoke to my heart.

I had been thinking of going to someone whose behavior had been adversely affecting a lot of people for a long time and who appeared to be getting away with it. I wanted to do something about it right then. But God wanted me to know at that time anyway that He did NOT want me to take on the job of confronting the person. He had a job for me to do but it wasn't that one. What I was thinking of doing was NOT His will then anyway. He wanted me to NOT get distracted. He wanted me to STAY FOCUSED. On Him and on His will for me. On the job He had given me.

Is this message for you, friend? Are you involved in something right now, or thinking of getting involved in something, that is not a job God has assigned you at least right now anyway? That is not His will for you at least right now? Seek, wait on, hear, and obey the Lord!

"You will keep *him* in perfect peace, *Whose* mind *is* stayed *on You,* Because he trusts in You." Isaiah 26:3 NKJV

…

#25

Heartbroken

Ever felt crushed? Heartbroken? I am sensitive. I feel stuff deeply. I am emotional. I have a humungous heart. My heart has been broken countless times over the years. Whether or not people intended it, so many times so many people have hurt me. And it didn't hurt just a little. With my big heart, with my sensitivity, oh how it hurt. Oh, how it still does when it happens. Heartbreak. Heartache. Ouch.

One day I felt so hurt by what some people did. Tears came. I felt crushed all over again. But this time I did something different. I didn't go to the world looking for comfort and a fix. I didn't build a big brick wall around my heart and determine to distance myself from people to not risk any further hurt. I didn't push God away. I didn't go hide under the covers. I didn't consider not moving forward with the day. I didn't think about not loving and serving the Lord with all my heart and loving and serving others in His name. I didn't hold any grudges toward the people. I didn't refuse to love them, forgive them, and pray for them as God calls us to do. I did something so simple. I went to the Lord. And prayed. A very simple prayer.

"I feel crushed," I told the Lord. "Take my heart in your hands and heal me." I prayed. Then I went on with my day.

This world offers a zillion ways to deal with hurt and heartbreak and heartache. I have tried many of them. Some have been negative and dangerous and even potentially deadly. Others seemed positive and helped some but the help was only temporary. I have since found the #1 and only 100% guaranteed fix for heartbreak.

THE LORD JESUS CHRIST and the Bible. Oh, sure, we can and should reach out to others as the Lord leads for love, comfort, prayer, and encouragement and support. But people are imperfect and the love, comfort, encouragement, prayer, and support we offer one another though wonderful and helpful can never measure up to the amazing and awesome love and comfort and blessedness and healing and fellowship of the Lord.

Heartbroken? Turn from your sins. Believe Jesus Christ is Lord and in His death and resurrection. Turn your life over truly once and for all to God and His ways. Receive His forgiveness and the promise of a forever relationship with Him. Be filled with His Holy Spirit. And whenever your heart breaks and aches, love and forgive those who have hurt you, pray for them as the Lord leads you, and seek and follow God's will regarding whether to stay in their lives or not and how to address any issues in your interaction with them.

Above all else, SPEND TIME ALONE WITH THE LORD POURING OUT YOUR HEART TO HIM, FINDING REST AND HEALING AND HOPE AND JOY AND FELLOWSHIP AND WISDOM AND COMFORT IN HIM, PUTTING YOUR TRUST IN HIM, COMMUNING WITH HIM, PRAYING TO HIM, SEEKING HIM, HEARING HIM, BASKING IN THE SUNSHINE OF HIS LOVE, ENJOYING HIS LOVE, PRAISING

AND WORSHIPING HIM, WHATEVER IT IS THE LORD PLACES ON YOUR HEART TO DO IN YOUR TIME ALONE WITH HIM, THEN CONTINUE ON WITH YOUR LIFE WITH THE LOVE OF JESUS FOR THE GLORY OF GOD, OH YES, AMEN!

"Grace to you and peace from God our Father and the Lord Jesus Christ. Blessed *be* the God and Father of our Lord Jesus Christ, the Father of mercies and God of all comfort, who comforts us in all our tribulation, that we may be able to comfort those who are in any trouble, with the comfort with which we ourselves are comforted by God. For as the sufferings of Christ abound in us, so our consolation also abounds through Christ. Now if we are afflicted, *it is* for your consolation and salvation, which is effective for enduring the same sufferings which we also suffer. Or if we are comforted, *it is* for your consolation and salvation." 2 Corinthians 1:2-6 NKJV

…

#26

I Am Mad!

"I am mad!" I declared. Not out loud. In my heart.

"Get the anger out of your heart," the Lord spoke to my heart. Immediately.

I was about to make a phone call. Years and years of not purifying my heart. Old habits die hard. Not just old habits. Old sin. Ugly, yucky, sin against God. I was going to get on the phone with an angry heart. And Lord only knew where I undoubtedly would be headed with my mouth.

I knew what I needed to do. Get rid of the anger. Forgive anyone and everyone I needed to forgive. Then pick up the phone and not bring a heart of sin into the conversation. But instead bring a heart filled with the love and light and hope and peace and joy and mercy of Jesus the Christ.

A fundamental necessity in being a Jesus follower is to continually purify our hearts, mouths, and actions so we're living in love for and obedience to the Lord!

I so wish I could tell you I never get on the phone angry anymore and I'm never mean and never mess up and all sin is behind me, but this is so not true. I am a work very much in progress, and I praise the Lord for His faithful love and amazing mercy with me as He patiently teaches me to walk in His ways.

Got any anger in your heart? Any meanness in your mouth? Anything in your heart, words, and actions that needs to be gotten rid of? Do you continually purify yourself for the Lord? Oh, please do!

"that you put off, concerning your former conduct, the old man which grows corrupt according to the deceitful lusts, and be renewed in the spirit of your mind, and that you put on the new man which was created according to God, in true righteousness and holiness. Therefore, putting away lying, "LET EACH ONE OF YOU SPEAK TRUTH WITH HIS NEIGHBOR," for we are members of one another. "BE ANGRY, AND DO NOT SIN": do not let the sun go down on your wrath, nor give place to the devil. Let him who stole steal no longer, but rather let him labor, working with *his* hands what is good, that he may have something to give him who has need. Let no corrupt word proceed out of your mouth, but what is good for necessary edification, that it may impart grace to the hearers. And do not grieve the Holy Spirit of God, by whom you were sealed for the day of redemption.

Let all bitterness, wrath, anger, clamor, and evil speaking be put away from you, with all malice. And be kind to one another, tenderhearted, forgiving one another, even as God in Christ forgave you." Ephesians 4:22-32 NKJV

…

#27

But God I'm Comfortable!

Did I ask you to call [so and so]?" the Lord spoke to my heart.

"Yes," I replied.

"Why aren't you?"

"Because I'm lying here and I'm comfortable," I said. I don't slow down all too often though I'm ever in need of rest, but when I do slow down I'm not exactly ready to move until I feel good and ready.

Ugh. The Lord didn't need to speak another word to my heart. His Holy Spirit brought conviction deep within.

I am the one who regularly tells people and writes about how Jesus' followers are to deny self, take up our crosses, and to follow Him. How we're not to live for self but for the Lord. How we're not to live to please ourselves and seek pleasure and comfort for me, me, and me. How instead we're to live to love and worship and glorify the Lord forever and to love others. Enough said.

I got up out of the bed to write this message and to make the call God wanted me to make.

For Christ's sake, let us humble ourselves, lay aside our comfort when God calls us to do so, and forsake all for the Lord. This doesn't mean we'll never be comfortable. It doesn't mean the Lord doesn't want to bless us and for us to enjoy our lives. But it does mean God and His will must come first and that the enjoyment and pleasure and comfort we do have must be God-ordained and pleasing and honoring to Him.

I've been on the road for Jesus with my special needs ministry dogs for some years now and have experienced quite a bit of leaving behind comfort for Christ both in small ways and big ways, and it's been worth leaving behind every ounce of comfort God has called me to forsake to enjoy the amazing blessedness of loving and serving the Lord and others with every ounce of my heart!

Any comfort God wants you to forsake to follow Him? Please don't argue. Please don't rebel against Him. Please turn it loose and be totally devoted to the Lord and His will for you each and every day and forever and ever, AMEN!

"Yet indeed I also count all things loss for the excellence of the knowledge of Christ Jesus my Lord, for whom I have suffered the loss of all things, and count them as rubbish, that I may gain Christ." Philippians 3:8 NKJV

"Then He said to *them* all, "If anyone desires to come after Me, let him deny himself, and take up his cross daily, and follow Me." Luke 9:23 NKJV

...

#28

I Want You Lord!

Early morning. My favorite time of day. Clean slate. Fresh start. Anything possible. So much potential. My mind already going full speed as it does through the night and at all times honestly. That's when passion burst forth in my heart. And these words came to mind. I told them to the Lord. Vehemently. "I want you Lord!"

No recollection of what I was thinking about at the time. But I do know this. Those words say everything about where the Lord has brought me in life and ministry. I love and adore and revere and desire to please, bring joy and pleasure to, make proud, honor, praise, sing to, worship, serve, obey, glorify, and tell others about the Lord more than anything or anyone on this earth. And I want the Lord and His Spirit and an ever-closer, ever-deeper, ever-more-intimate relationship with Him more than I want any person, place, or thing I could have for the rest of my life. I am madly, passionately, head-over-heels, immeasurably, unfathomably, unimaginably in love with the Lord and His Word.

Perhaps surprisingly to you, and it most assuredly is to me, I am a 100% Jewish follower of the Lord Jesus Christ who for decades was broken beyond human hope and repair and who was an atheist at one time not to mention immersed in all sorts of false religious beliefs along the way. Not to mention for a long time after I came to believe in Jesus Christ as Lord I ran the gamut of spiritually dead, apathetic, lukewarm, consumed with self not Christ, etc. But the Lord didn't leave me where I was. He brought me to where I am!

I wouldn't go back to my old life and heart for anything in the world. There is nothing more wonderful, fulfilling, satisfying, exciting, joyful, life-giving, life-changing, amazing, awesome, and phenomenal in the universe than God almighty and having a forever relationship with Him instead of spending eternity in hell and the lake of fire in forever torment apart from Him.

I encourage you with all my heart to turn from your sins, believe in Jesus Christ as Lord and in His death and resurrection, sincerely commit your heart and life to God and His ways, receive God's forgiveness and the promise of forever with Him and the indwelling of His Holy Spirit, and become and remain TOTALLY DEVOTED to the Lord Jesus Christ now and forevermore.

There is nothing and nobody we should love more and treat as a higher priority than the Lord and loving and serving Him with every ounce of our hearts today, tomorrow, and forever and ever, AMEN!

Who and what do you want more than anything else in the universe? May your answer be THE LORD and being TOTALLY DEVOTED TO HIM forevermore! Hallelujah!

If you need help beginning or continuing on in a forever relationship with the Lord, feel free to reach out at 843-338-2219 or lara@GoodNews.love.

"As the deer pants for the water brooks, So pants my soul for You, O God. My soul thirsts for God, for the living God. When shall I come and appear before God?" Psalms 42:1-2 NKJV

""I know your works, that you are neither cold nor hot. I could wish you were cold or hot. So then, because you are lukewarm, and neither cold nor hot, I will vomit you out of My mouth." Revelation 3:15-16 NKJV

...

#29

Making God Happy

I was up in the middle of the night as I often am spending time with the Lord without the usual distractions and busyness of the day when these words came to me. I was too tired to get out of bed and go to my computer, so I simply grabbed a pen and wrote them down on the closest thing to paper I could find. The side of my tissue box. There the words were the next morning to remind me of this message that is near and dear to my heart. Making God Happy.

For most of my life thus far, I have done what the world teaches us to do. Seek happiness no matter the cost to achieve it. Today, a totally devoted follower of the Lord Jesus Christ, at long last I am living the way God intended us all to live. For Him. And for others. Which brings me to this. What if we all stopped living to make ourselves happy and started living to make God happy? What would our hearts and lives look like? What would this world look like? What would YOUR life look like?

What if each and every day you lived to make God happy? To love, praise, adore, revere, honor, fear, obey, serve, worship, and glorify the Lord no matter the cost to self? Would your life look different than it is right now? Are you ready to make any and all changes God wants you to make in order to make Him happy? Are you ready to live utterly for the Lord?

Friend, I wouldn't go back to living for self for anything in the world. I find no greater joy than in the Lord and than in loving and serving Him with all my heart, loving others as myself, and striving to make God happy. Even writing this brings a smile to my heart and face.

Please, I implore you, do what Jesus tells us to do. Deny self, take up your cross, and follow the Lord. Make God happy. I believe with all my heart there is no fleeting worldly happiness that can compare to the joy of Jesus and living for Him! Amen!

"Then He said to *them* all, "If anyone desires to come after Me, let him deny himself, and take up his cross daily, and follow Me." Luke 9:23 NKJV

#30

The Man Who Listened to Me

How refreshed and relatively shocked I was when a business man with whom I crossed paths took the love, time, and care to listen to me about a certain very concerning matter. Not only did he listen, but he had every intention of addressing the issues I brought to his attention. Maybe this isn't a big deal for you, but it is for me. I have a background strongly impacted by the fact when I needed help with something very big nobody wanted to listen and help, and I have seen this in our world countless times. Whereby people want to pretend bad stuff isn't happening and so they look the other way and go on with their lives all the while people are being hurt, taken advantage of, neglected, abused, trodden over, treated as invisible, disregarded, accused of making things up, etc.

Why am I bringing this to your attention? At the end of the day we will all stand before the Lord and have to give an account of our lives. Can you imagine if the Lord points out all the times in our lives He wanted us to help someone, to love someone, to listen to someone, to support someone, to give to someone, to pray for someone, to encourage someone, to report something to authorities and professionals etc. about someone in trouble, in need, etc., and when instead we looked the other way and shoved what we heard and saw under the rug so we could go on with our own lives in comfort and ease?

Ouch, I feel conviction even as I write this. The conviction that we all have a job to do on this earth. To love and serve the Lord with all our hearts and to love others as ourselves. We are to believe in Jesus Christ as Lord and in His death and resurrection and to follow Jesus Christ as Lord and to

LIVE FOR JESUS CHRIST AS LORD. This means when God leads us to someone in need He wants us to help in any way, shape, or form, we should humble ourselves, listen and love, and do whatever God desires to help.

Please don't turn the other way. Please don't walk away. Please don't run away. Seems a rare commodity in this day and age, but may you and I be people who obey the Lord in all things – including when it comes to listening and helping a world in need, AMEN!

Please note in the so-called Good Samaritan story that follows how only one man stopped everything he was doing to go all out helping the person in need. The others turned away. Which one will you and I be? The Lord will make known whom He wants us to help. Let us do so with His love, in His strength, with the resources He gives us, with His mercy and grace, by the power of His Holy Spirit who lives inside His followers, in His name, for the glory of the Lord, AMEN!

"And behold, a certain lawyer stood up and tested Him, saying, "Teacher, what shall I do to inherit eternal life?" He said to him, "What is written in the law? What is your reading *of it?*" So he answered and said, "'YOU SHALL LOVE THE LORD YOUR GOD WITH ALL YOUR HEART, WITH ALL YOUR SOUL, WITH ALL YOUR STRENGTH, AND WITH ALL YOUR MIND,' and 'YOUR NEIGHBOR AS YOURSELF.'" And He said to him, "You have answered rightly; do this and you will live." But he, wanting to justify himself, said to Jesus, "And who is my neighbor?" Then Jesus answered and said: "A certain *man* went down from Jerusalem to Jericho, and fell among thieves, who stripped him of his clothing, wounded *him,* and departed, leaving *him* half dead. Now by chance a certain priest came down that road. And when he saw him, he passed by on the other side. Likewise a Levite, when he arrived at the place, came and looked, and passed by on the other side. But a certain Samaritan, as he journeyed, came where he was. And when he saw him, he had compassion. So he went to *him* and bandaged his wounds, pouring on oil and wine; and he set him on his own animal, brought him to an inn, and took care of him. On the next day, when he departed, he took out two denarii, gave *them* to the innkeeper, and said to him, 'Take care of him; and whatever more you spend, when I come again, I will repay you.' So which of these three do you think was neighbor to him who fell among the thieves?" And he said, "He who showed mercy on him." Then Jesus said to him, "Go and do likewise."'" Luke 10:25-37 NKJV

...

#31

The Worst Neglect Case Ever

When I was a school girl, a girl who went to my school was found locked in a closet eating her own feces due to child neglect and abuse. Decades later, I still remember the awfulness and heinousness of what that poor child had been found to be going through. Neglecting children is awful, and that particular case was one of the most extreme cases I have personally heard of. But neglect doesn't stop with children, nor does the awfulness of neglect.

Neglecting elderly people is awful. Neglecting loved ones is awful. Neglecting people in need is awful. Neglecting widows and orphans whom the Lord has such a heart for is awful. Neglecting the sick, injured, hurting, dying, depressed, homeless, hungry, poor, struggling any time God calls us to love and help and support and encourage and pray for them is awful. Neglecting animals entrusted to us is awful. But there is no neglect in the world more awful than neglecting God almighty. And some of us are doing just that.

Countless people worldwide are neglecting to turn from their sins, to believe in Jesus Christ as Lord and in His death and resurrection, to turn their lives over to God and His ways, to receive His forgiveness and the promise of forever life with Him, and to live going forward for the Lord according to His ways. These people are neglecting God in what we may consider to be the worst of ways, but let me ask you this. What about all those professing to believe in Jesus Christ as Lord and calling themselves Christians and neglecting God each and every day? This is neglect also, isn't it, and the worst neglect of all is when any of us on this earth neglect God almighty in any way, shape, or form.

I was studying the Book of Revelation in the middle of one night when I noticed how Jesus tells the churches – essentially the Body of Christ, or believers in Him – they need to repent. In three cases, He points to neglect. First, some have left their first love! They are DOING good things for God, it seems, but apparently they have abandoned God Himself! In the second, the people seem to be alive but in fact apparently are spiritually dead! In the third, the people are "lukewarm" about God which Jesus despises. He is warning us against all three kinds of neglect, but neglect doesn't stop with just this, does it?

God commands us to love Him with all our hearts, souls, minds, and strength. He is to be number one in our lives. But truth is many, many believers right now in this world are paying little to no attention to the Lord, to the Bible, and to God's will for our lives. I meet countless people even churchgoing people who seem to have no care for God Himself, for reading and living by the Bible, for being filled with and led by God's Holy Spirit, for denying self, taking up their crosses, and for following Jesus day by day and forevermore. For being totally devoted to the Lord Jesus Christ as we should be.

Friend, I neglected God for a long time until the Lord set me straight. For some time, I didn't know better because I didn't have people around me helping me to follow the Lord. Then, for some time, I was under false teaching. But even when God delivered me from false teaching, I still neglected God to a degree. Today, by God's grace alone, I am a totally devoted follower of the Lord Jesus Christ.

There is nobody in the universe more important than the Lord. There is nothing in the universe more important than loving, praising, worshiping, serving, obeying, praying to, adoring, spending time alone with, meditating on, talking about, singing to, serving, and glorifying the Lord God almighty.

God is to be our first love. The Lord is to be our highest priority. He is to be our number one. Living to love and glorify Him is to be our greatest desire. Loving Him and bringing Him joy, honor, praise, adoration, pleasure and glory is to be at the top of our to-do list. Being alone with Him daily in His presence, experiencing and enjoying and being transformed by and drawing ever closer to Him is to be more important than anything else. And being solidly planted in the Body of Christ loving and serving one another and helping one another to follow Him and to grow in relationship with Him and to tell others about Him, etc. is to be a fundamental part of our lives.

If we find we are neglecting the Lord, nothing should be more important than repenting of any and all neglect and making God our first love and highest priority.

This message may be hard to read. It's hard to write. But I am so very compelled to share it with you. May the Lord use it mightily to bring conviction, chastening, and change that more and more people around the world would become and remain totally devoted followers of the Lord Jesus Christ, AMEN!

"Jesus said to him, 'YOU SHALL LOVE THE LORD YOUR GOD WITH ALL YOUR HEART, WITH ALL YOUR SOUL, AND WITH ALL YOUR MIND.'" Matthew 22:37 NKJV

""I know your works, your labor, your patience, and that you cannot bear those who are evil. And you have tested those who say they are apostles and are not, and have found them liars; and you have persevered and have patience, and have labored for My name's sake and have not become weary. Nevertheless I have *this* against you, that you have left your first love. Remember therefore from where you have fallen; repent and do the first works, or else I will come to you quickly and remove your lampstand from its place—unless you repent." Revelation 2:2-5 NKJV

""And to the angel of the church in Sardis write, 'These things says He who has the seven Spirits of God and the seven stars: "I know your works, that you have a name that you are alive, but you are dead. Be watchful, and strengthen the things which remain, that are ready to die, for I have not found your works perfect before God. Remember therefore how you have received and heard; hold fast and repent. Therefore if you will not watch, I will come upon you as a thief, and you will not know what hour I will come upon you. You have a few names even in Sardis who have not defiled their garments; and they shall walk with Me in white, for they are worthy." Revelation 3:1-4 NKJV

""I know your works, that you are neither cold nor hot. I could wish you were cold or hot. So then, because you are lukewarm, and neither cold nor hot, I will vomit you out of My mouth. Because you say, 'I am rich, have become wealthy, and have need of nothing'—and do not know that you are wretched, miserable, poor, blind, and naked— I counsel you to buy from Me gold refined in the fire, that you may be rich; and white garments, that you may be clothed, *that* the shame of your nakedness may not be revealed; and anoint your eyes with eye salve, that you may see. As many as I love, I rebuke and chasten. Therefore be zealous and repent." Revelation 3:15-19 NKJV

"And you have forgotten the exhortation which speaks to you as to sons: "MY SON, DO NOT DESPISE THE CHASTENING OF THE LORD, NOR BE DISCOURAGED WHEN YOU ARE REBUKED BY HIM; FOR WHOM THE LORD LOVES HE CHASTENS, AND SCOURGES EVERY SON WHOM HE RECEIVES." If you endure chastening, God deals with you as with sons; for what son is there whom a father does not chasten? But if you are without chastening, of which all have become partakers, then you are illegitimate and not sons. Furthermore, we have had human fathers who corrected *us,* and we paid *them* respect. Shall we not much more readily be in subjection to the Father of spirits and live? For they indeed for a few days chastened *us* as seemed *best* to them, but He for *our* profit, that *we* may be partakers of His holiness. Now no chastening seems to be joyful for the present, but painful; nevertheless, afterward it yields the peaceable fruit of righteousness to those who have been trained by it." Hebrews 12:5-11 NKJV

"Then He said to *them* all, "If anyone desires to come after Me, let him deny himself, and take up his cross daily, and follow Me." Luke 9:23 NKJV

…

#32

The Woman Outside My Door

I was having so much trouble focusing. So often do these days. I had so much work to do. But so distracted. Bouncing around from one thing to another. Couldn't sit still. That's when I saw the woman outside my door. At my latest hotel on the road for Jesus. Now please understand before you proceed with this message. It's not about me and what I did. I don't even want to tell you. But I am compelled to do so because I have an important message to share with you in so doing. Not about the woman. Nor me. But about Jesus and this world.

I opened my hotel room door. There stood the woman. Visibly cold. Quiet. Still. She barely moved. Strange. With my noisy door, I would have thought she would be startled and move out of the way. Somewhere. Anywhere. But she stood right there which in retrospect I believe was because the Lord had sent her right by my door. I tried to speak to her. No English. Barely anyway. But I could see she was in need. No idea if she was staying at the hotel. Or why she was there. She seemed to be waiting for a ride somewhere. But God knew she needed more than the ride.

I used my hands and tried with my words to ask her if she needed something to make her warm. She answered quickly. Most people are too proud. She was quiet and humble. Yes, yes. To make a long story short, within about 15 minutes, I had the great privilege of giving her a big super warm wonderful beautiful pullover I had gotten for myself at a thrift shop I had really wanted for myself. I had worn it only once or twice. It was clearly not for me. It was for her.

I got her a cup of coffee, some snacks, some tissues as she seemed on the verge of tears or perhaps just so cold. She seemed sad. Oh, and yes, most important of all. I pointed upward to the Lord. And said "Jesus" the way Spanish speaking people do. She seemed to believe in Him. I prayed for her. With tears, I prayed. For this beautiful quiet woman God had sent to my door. By the end of our brief time together, she stood elsewhere waiting for her ride with her warm pullover, coffee, snacks, tissues, LOVE, and PRAYED FOR.

And I went back to my room and felt ready to cry for this whole world filled with so much suffering and need. Need of Jesus. And need of people who will stop everything they're doing and humble ourselves before God almighty, and turn from our sins and believe in Jesus Christ as Lord and in His death and resurrection, truly turning to God and His ways, receiving God's forgiveness and the promise of forever life with Him, being indwelt by His Holy Spirit. Willing and desirous and committed to living henceforth for the Lord according to His ways.

Loving and serving Him with all our hearts and ever being ready to share the Gospel message, to love with the love of Jesus, to serve in His name, to give, sacrifice, share, pray for, encourage, help, support, to obey God in anything and everything to which He calls us day by day. Including in the way of proclaiming His name and sharing His love with a world in dire need of Him.

I ask only one thing as you finish reading this message. Please don't put me on a pedestal for my heart for Jesus and ministry and people and special needs dogs and such. Please don't look at me and exalt me in any way for I am nothing and nobody without Jesus. But please become and remain a totally devoted follower of the Lord Jesus Christ and go out into this world and love and serve Him and others with every ounce of your heart, AMEN!

""When the Son of Man comes in His glory, and all the holy angels with Him, then He will sit on the throne of His glory. All the nations will be gathered before Him, and He will separate them one from another, as a shepherd divides *his* sheep from the goats. And He will set the sheep on His right hand, but the goats on the left. Then the King will say to those on His right hand, 'Come, you blessed of My Father, inherit the kingdom prepared for you from the foundation of the world: for I was hungry and you gave Me food; I was thirsty and you gave Me drink; I was a stranger and you took Me in; I *was* naked and you clothed Me; I was sick and you visited Me; I was in prison and you came to Me.' "Then the righteous will answer Him, saying, 'Lord, when did we see You hungry and feed *You,* or thirsty and give *You* drink? When did we see You a stranger and take *You* in, or naked and clothe *You?* Or when did we see You sick, or in prison, and come to You?' And the King will answer and say to them, 'Assuredly, I say to you, inasmuch as you did *it* to one of the least of these My brethren, you did *it* to Me.' "Then He will also say to those on the left hand, 'Depart from Me, you cursed, into the everlasting fire prepared for the devil and his angels: for I was hungry and you gave Me no food; I was thirsty and you gave Me no drink; I was a stranger and you did not take Me in, naked and you did not clothe Me, sick and in prison and you did not visit Me.' "Then they also will answer Him, saying, 'Lord, when did we see You hungry or thirsty or a stranger or naked or sick or in prison, and did not minister to You?' Then He will answer them, saying, 'Assuredly, I say to you, inasmuch as you did not do *it* to one of the least of these, you did not do *it* to Me.' And these will

go away into everlasting punishment, but the righteous into eternal life.""
Matthew 25:31-46 NKJV

...

#33

Bring Your Heart to God

Angry? Sad? Hurt? Joyful? Happy? Scared? Worried? Doubting? Bitter?
Feeling vengeful? Depressed? Anxiety attacks? Grieving? Irritated?
Discouraged? Elated? Passionate? Lonely? One thing I have learned to do
with emotions that has been such an exceeding blessing from God is to take
all of my emotions to Him. To pour out my heart to Him. ALL of my heart.
No matter my feelings. To bring them all to Him. To commune with Him.
To spend time alone in His presence. To tell Him how I feel. To cast ALL
my feelings upon Him. To repent of any thoughts, feelings, words, and
actions displeasing to Him. And with ALL my feelings, to give them ALL
to Him. I am His child. I am His servant. I am His follower.

I learn day by day to put my trust in Him and to put my heart in His
blessed almighty powerful beautiful sovereign hands. And even as I do this,
I draw closer to Him and He draws closer to me. And He brings me His
love, hope, mercy, forgiveness, grace, comfort, healing, wisdom, direction,
friendship, fellowship, more and more intimacy with Him, as He grows me
and draws me ever closer to Himself.

Please, friend, bring your heart to the Lord Jesus Christ. And watch when
you turn from your sins, believe in Him as Lord and in His death and
resurrection, turning your life over to God and His ways, receiving His
forgiveness and the promise of forever with Him, His Holy Spirit coming to

live inside you, learning to follow Him day by day, what the Lord will do when you surrender your heart and life utterly to Him. Oh, bring your heart to the Lord, AMEN!

"Trust in Him at all times, you people; Pour out your heart before Him; God *is* a refuge for us. Selah" Psalms 62:8 NKJV

…

#34

God Caught Me

One night God caught me starting to do something I wasn't supposed to be doing. Now you not might think it was awful or anything, but the reality was God had made clear I needed to not go down an old pathway He had mercifully taken me off of. There I was headed right back down it when He caught me – and stopped me. And swiftly led me to repentance.

Oh, thank God for His love and mercy, His grace and forgiveness, His kindness and patience, His ever working on His children to perfect His ways in us!

We don't see God in the flesh standing in front of us, and He doesn't walk around in human form everywhere we go, and He doesn't sit down with us at the dinner table or hunt us down in the wrong places we go, or drive with us in our cars, or come to work with us, not in human flesh anyway. But the Spirit of God who lives inside His followers knows good and well everything we think, feel, say, and do.

And the Holy Spirit in His love for us will bring conviction, chastening, and correction and lead us to repentance when we need it. That night, God caught me before I went any further in the wrong direction.

Question is, how will we respond when God catches, convicts, chastens, and corrects us?

Will we humble ourselves and repent? Or in our pride and wickedness walk on down the pathway of wickedness, ungodliness, and unrighteousness?

Let us yield ourselves to the Holy Spirit of God and be thankful that in His love for us He leads us down the pathway of righteousness, godliness, and holiness. And let us humbly, lovingly, reverently follow Him as He leads us forth. Amen!

"He leads me in the paths of righteousness For His name's sake." Psalms 23:3 NKJV

"My son, do not despise the chastening of the LORD, Nor detest His correction; For whom the LORD loves He corrects, Just as a father the son *in whom* he delights." Proverbs 3:11-12 NKJV

…

#35

Don't Leave If

Don't leave that person, place, or thing you're thinking of leaving if God doesn't tell you to leave. This message is for someone reading this, I am quite sure. Maybe even many. Your flesh may be screaming to RUN, to make a quick exit, to say goodbye for now, or goodbye for good, to hit the road, to quit the job, to end a relationship, to sign those papers ending it, etc.

But DON'T LEAVE if God isn't leading you to do so. He will give you the love, mercy, grace, forgiveness, strength, resources, help, support, wisdom, counsel, helpers, whatever it is He knows you need to stay and not leave if it is not His will for you to go.

Turn from your sins, believe Jesus Christ is Lord and in His death and resurrection, commit yourself 100% to God and His ways, receive His forgiveness and the promise of forever life with Him and the indwelling of His Holy Spirit, become totally devoted to the Lord, cry out to Him, seek Him, pray to Him, read the Bible, get support from followers of Jesus, wait on God, hear God, and obey God.

If He is not telling you to leave, remain where He wants you. Unless and until He says otherwise, be faithful to the Lord. Humble yourself before Him, put your trust in Him, and press on. In the strength of Christ, for the glory of Christ, AMEN!

"I can do all things through Christ who strengthens me." Philippians 4:13 NKJV

…

#36

What Would Jesus NOT Do?

You've probably heard the expression, "What would Jesus do?" If I'm not mistaken, it comes from one of my all-time favorite books, IN HIS STEPS by Charles Sheldon. Needless to say, thinking about what Jesus WOULD do in a situation, praying to God to show us, studying the Bible so we do know, and DOING what Jesus would do, in other words what God's will is, is crucial in the life of a Jesus follower. That said, we should also pay attention to what Jesus would NOT do – and make sure we do NOT do it either!

If we find we have already done something Jesus would NOT do, or are currently doing something Jesus would NOT do, we should repent and turn to the Lord and do what Jesus would do. And if we have not yet done what Jesus would NOT do, we should make sure we don't do it! Plain and simple, we who believe in Jesus should follow Jesus and in following Jesus should obey the Lord!

Examples of what Jesus would NOT do? Hurt people who are hurting Him, lash out at people who lash out at Him, hate people who hate Him, live for self, pick and choose whom to love, live for pleasure, go against the Bible, turn His back on widows and orphans, feel sorry for Himself, be led by His feelings instead of by the Holy Spirit, brag about Himself, be prideful, be impatient, be rude, be condescending, be controlling and manipulative, be dishonest, be greedy and gluttonous, lose His temper at people as a result of not getting what He wants, hurt the heart of God the Father, trample over people to get what He wants, etc.

So here is the question. Is there anything you and I are doing that Jesus would NOT do? Let us go before the Lord regularly, let us purify our hearts and lives regularly, let us repent regularly, and let us be committed to being totally devoted followers of the Lord Jesus Christ, AMEN!

"and He died for all, that those who live should live no longer for themselves, but for Him who died for them and rose again." 2 Corinthians 5:15 NKJV

"Therefore be imitators of God as dear children. And walk in love, as Christ also has loved us and given Himself for us, an offering and a sacrifice to God for a sweet-smelling aroma." Ephesians 5:1-2 NKJV

...

#37

Negativity? An Awesome Alternative

I have been prone to negativity for as long as I can remember. If you know me now that I am a totally devoted follower of the Lord Jesus Christ, maybe you would not believe it. Promise you, it is true. But negativity is sin and hurts God and others and ironically doesn't do an ounce of good for us despite how the flesh may find temporary pleasure in it. I strive hard now to not fall into negativity and to repent quickly when I do. One day the Lord brought to my heart something awesome about the temptation to be negative. An awesome alternative.

When we resist the temptation to be negative, we have an amazing opportunity – TO PRAY!

Examples? A group of homeless alcoholics and addicts are making lots of noise and mess at a local park. Don't be negative. Pray for them. The local prison is overflowing with criminals who have been wreaking havoc on your beloved town. Don't be negative. Pray for them. Pray for the town officials. Pray for your neighbors. It's been raining and cold for weeks and you are so tired of being inside all the time. Don't be negative. Take the extra time to pray.

Your employer is nasty, your co-workers are anything but kind, your company is falling apart, and you know for now God wants you to stay at this job. Don't be negative. Pray for them all. And pray for God to use the trial to grow you.

The television news is so incredibly negative. Everything in the world seems to be falling apart. Don't be negative about the negative news. Pray for the world. Pray about the situations. Pray for the government. Pray for the people you hear about in the news. Pray for those you know and those you don't, pray, pray, pray.

Everything in your world seems to be falling apart. Don't be negative. Pray for God's will. Pray for His strength. Pray for help. Pray for God to carry you through it all. Pray for His forgiveness for any wrongdoing. Pray for wisdom. Pray for discernment. Pray for direction. Pray for comfort. Pray for a deeper, stronger relationship with the Lord. Pray, yes, pray.

Above all else, pray God would sent laborers out to share the Gospel, pray God would give you the courage to share the Gospel, pray God would lead people to repentance and faith in Him, pray for those turned away from Him to return to Him, pray for lukewarm believers to be on fire for the Lord, pray people worldwide would humble themselves and commit their lives to the Lord Jesus Christ, and pray as often as the Lord leads you for anything or anyone anywhere in this world from the people in the room where you are right now to people across the world. Pray however the Lord leads you to pray. Whenever He leads you to pray. Yield to the Holy Spirit who lives inside His followers as He leads you who follow Him to pray. Oh, yes, pray!

Don't be negative! Pray!

"Pray without ceasing." 1 Thess. 5:17

"Then He said to them, "The harvest truly *is* great, but the laborers *are* few; therefore pray the Lord of the harvest to send out laborers into His harvest." Luke 10:2 NKJV

...

#38

How NOT to Handle Hurt

Someone has been hurting me for DECADES. Not only is the hurt exceeding, and not only will the wounds and scars be with me until I draw my last breath, but the person in her pride has never once acknowledged her wrongdoing nor made any loving change. What she has done, and is doing, and how if I bring the subject up she twists it around and lashes out at me, has done permanent damage. But this message isn't about what SHE has done wrong. It's about how NOT to handle hurt.

Recently [as of the writing of this message] I fell back into sin in response to her wrongdoing. I meditated on how she treats me, got really riled up about it, lost my temper, and lashed out in vengeance foolishly thinking somehow despite years of trying to show her how she hurts me that this time around I would have an impact and she would apologize and change. In typical fashion, she turned it around and blamed me. But this isn't the point. I SHOULD NOT HAVE LOST MY TEMPER, LASHED OUT, TAKEN MY ANGER OUT ON HER, AND TRIED TO CHANGE HER.

One of the most powerful verses in the Bible when it comes to how to handle hurt for me is about the Lord Jesus Christ:

"For to this you were called, because Christ also suffered for us, leaving us an example, that you should follow His steps: "WHO COMMITTED NO SIN, NOR WAS DECEIT FOUND IN HIS MOUTH"; who, when He was reviled, did not revile in return; when He suffered, He did not threaten, but committed *Himself* to Him who judges righteously; who Himself bore our sins in His own body on the tree, that we, having died to sins, might live for righteousness—by whose stripes you were healed." 1 Peter 2:21-24 NKJV

God mercifully led me to repentance. I sought His forgiveness and hers. She of course did not apologize for what she has done all these years. But that's not the point. We who follow Jesus are to love, forgive, and to be merciful. Sometimes God will call us to walk away from relationships with people who hurt us, and sometimes He will call us to stay. But either way, we need to obey God. And NOT seek vengeance, NOT hurt those hurting us, NOT act out of our emotions, etc. We are to "walk in love".

I have the strongest sense as I write this that someone or even many people who read it really need to hear this. Do you?

"But if you do not forgive men their trespasses, neither will your Father forgive your trespasses." Matthew 6:15

"Beloved, do not avenge yourselves, but *rather* give place to wrath; for it is written, "VENGEANCE IS MINE, I WILL REPAY," says the Lord." Romans 12:19

"Therefore be imitators of God as dear children. And walk in love, as Christ also has loved us and given Himself for us, an offering and a sacrifice to God for a sweet-smelling aroma." Ephesians 5:1-2 NKJV

By God's grace only, some time after writing this message, I noticed and was so blessedly thankful for a huge change regarding this person and the issue I shared with you. Is the person perfect? No! Will the person go back to what hurt so much? Maybe, maybe not. Am I perfect? I think of myself as the worst of all sinners! Remember, friend, though I was blessed by God and the person to see this change at least for a time, this message isn't about the other person. It's about how you and I handle hurt. Let us do so with godliness. Let us do so in a way glorifying to God and whereby the people who hurt us and others also see the love and grace of God in and through us, AMEN!

. . .

#39

Give God the Hurt

"I give you all the hurt," I told the Lord early one morning. Then this message came to me. GIVE GOD THE HURT.

I get hurt on a regular basis. Truth, people don't treat me so well. Oh, yes, some do. But I seem to be a magnet for people who aren't so good to me. I won't go into details. Suffice it to say I'm sensitive to begin with, and given the state of this world and the great lack of love in it, given my love for the Lord and for telling the world about Him, given my background and ongoing challenging circumstances, and given I seem to be a good doormat and scapegoat for people who aren't so kind, I know all about hurt. And to be transparent, I have done plenty of hurting others, plenty of repenting, and strive hard now to love and not hurt people. And praise the God almighty I have found the answer to being hurt.

LOVE. FORGIVE. PRAY. And be sure to GIVE GOD THE HURT. When people hurt us, we are to love them, forgive them, pray to God about the situation including about whether to stay in their lives, whether to confront them, what we may need to change, etc., and to pray for them as the Lord leads us. This we should do! But there is something else we can do that for a long time I really didn't understand but now do.

GIVE GOD THE HURT. We can pour our hearts out to God. We can come into His presence with our hurting hearts. We can tell Him how we feel. We can place our broken hearts in His hands. We can cry out to Him to heal us. We can ask for and receive His comfort. We can experience and enjoy His love. We can open the Bible and take comfort and find healing in His Word. We can ask Him for wisdom going forward and be thankful to Him when He gives it to us. We can hand our hurt off to Him. Then go on with our lives.

I felt such relief after giving God my hurt. Oh, sure, I felt better. But most importantly of all, God's greatest commands are to love Him with all our hearts and to love others as ourselves (Mark 12:30-31). When we're consumed with our hurt, we're consumed with self not the Lord Jesus Christ and others. When we give God our hurt, not only do we experience relief and freedom and healing, but we are best able to follow God's commands and to be available to the maximum to love Him with all our hearts, to love others as ourselves, and to fulfill His will, His plan, His purpose for our individual lives.

Oh, friend, give God the hurt! Amen!

"Trust in Him at all times, you people; Pour out your heart before Him; God *is* a refuge for us. Selah" Psalms 62:8 NKJV

…

#40

Why Should I Do This God?

Why? I asked God. He had just told me to do something. I wanted to know why. I deserved to know why. Before I obeyed. I should understand. God should explain Himself to me. Right?

Absolutely WRONG. Friend, we may never know why God tells us to do something. We may never understand. Or God may tell us. He may show us. He may reveal His reasons why. But our obedience to God should NOT be contingent on whether or not God tells us why, whether or not we understand, whether or not we like what God tells us to do, etc.

Our obedience should be contingent on this. Jesus Christ is Lord, and we are to humble ourselves and love, serve, obey, praise, worship, honor, revere, fear, adore, and glorify God with all our hearts because the Lord is God forever, AMEN!

Jesus tells us those who love Him are to obey Him. Let us humble ourselves before God almighty and do both. Let us love Him! Let us obey Him! And let us rejoice that Jesus Christ is Lord forevermore, Hallelujah, AMEN!

"If you love Me, keep My commandments." John 14:15 NKJV

"Trust in the LORD with all your heart, And lean not on your own understanding; In all your ways acknowledge Him, And He shall direct your paths." Proverbs 3:5-6 NKJV

...

#41

The Question I Asked My DOG

"Is everything worth wagging about?" I basically asked my special needs ministry dog Gracie one morning. Yes, I talk to my dogs.

That morning there was Gracie, years ago dumped at a gas station and hit by two cars before God sent her into my life, wagging her tail for the umpteenth time over the years for seemingly nothing. Like she could find a zillion reasons in her dog's life to be thankful and joyful about. Right down to the very, very simplest of things. To express her thanksgiving for. To wag her tail about. She finds so much to be thankful for and joyful over, and she makes sure to express her thanksgiving with that tail wagging, wagging, wagging!

What about you and me? Are we thankful to God and joyful in the Lord on an ongoing basis? Do we express our thanksgiving to Him regularly? No matter the trials of this life, do we "wag our tails" continually as we remember how wonderful and marvelous and glorious and splendorous and magnificent God is, how good He is, how much He blesses us each and every day? Are our hearts filled with thanksgiving to God and our mouths filled with praise of Him? Are we joyful in our hearts, attitudes, and is our joy evident in our actions and contagious to others?

My dog Gracie has no trouble finding something worth wagging her tail about. The Lord God almighty is worthy of praise, honor, thanksgiving, and joy forever, and should we not praise and thank and rejoice in Him this day and forevermore? Oh, yes!

"Make a joyful shout to the LORD, all you lands! Serve the LORD with gladness; Come before His presence with singing. Know that the LORD, He *is* God; *It is* He *who* has made us, and not we ourselves; *We are* His people and the sheep of His pasture. Enter into His gates with thanksgiving, *And* into His courts with praise. Be thankful to Him, *and* bless His name. For the LORD *is* good; His mercy *is* everlasting, And His truth *endures* to all generations." Psalms 100:1-5 NKJV

I encourage you to read the Bible each and every day, to live by it, and in your reading to pay attention to the exceeding number of references to the praise, honor, worship, thanksgiving, adoration, and glory God is worthy of and to which we are called to give unto Him!

"I will bless the LORD at all times; His praise *shall* continually *be* in my mouth." Psalms 34:1 NKJV

…

#42

Please Give God 100%

"I don't know why I am doing this," I thought.

I had a big project I had begun working on, and for all intents and purposes, it seemed pointless to do it. All projects like this one I had worked on in the past seemed to have failed. I had a zillion other things I could have been working on instead of this project. I was exhausted. I wasn't excited about it as perhaps I would have been under different circumstances and with seeming success in the past. So why was I committed to proceed with the project anyway?

THE LORD JESUS CHRIST. I have learned to give the Lord 100%. Because He is Lord. Because I am His. Because I love Him with all my heart. Because I don't need to understand why God tells me to do something. Because I don't need to feel like doing it. Because I don't need to get the results I want and not get the results I don't want. I do it above all else because Jesus Christ is Lord. Is my flesh pleased and comfortable and happy and at ease with all God calls me to do? No! Oh, but the joy I find in Jesus, in His love, in loving and serving Him with every ounce of my heart!

No matter what God calls you to do, please give Him the 100% He is worthy of in all He calls you to do for Him! Love and serve the Lord with every ounce of your heart, AMEN! With love, joy, gladness, and thanksgiving, serve the Lord, Hallelujah!

"Serve the LORD with gladness;…" Psalms 100:2

. . .

#43

Please God Help Us Not Run!

"God, please help her not to run," I prayed to God concerning someone I felt compelled to pray briefly for early one morning. "Except into your arms," I added to my simple prayer. I trusted God would answer.

I knew the woman was at high risk of running from a certain situation in which case she would be going against the will of God. She needed to remain if she were to be in obedience to the Lord.

Why do I share this with you? Because of what I had felt strongly compelled to add to my prayer. And how it may apply to you and me.

We may at times in our lives when we face various trials be tempted to run at high speed away from certain circumstances, relationships, situations, etc. God has clearly called us into. But instead of running from God's will for us, we should run TO THE LORD to pray, to pour out our hearts to Him, and for the love, strength, comfort, mercy, grace, forgiveness, hope, joy, peace, wisdom, fellowship, friendship, refreshing, renewal, restoration, healing, rest, etc. we need in order to be steadfast and faithful and to remain in His will.

In the Lord Jesus Christ, through Him, and for Him, we can find all we need to humbly, lovingly, reverently obey the Lord in all things. Let us not run away from that to which and to whom the Lord calls us. Let us run to

Him for all we need to love and serve Him with all our hearts as we learn to live in obedience to Him now and forevermore, hallelujah! Amen!

"According as his divine power hath given unto us all things that pertain unto life and godliness, through the knowledge of him that hath called us to glory and virtue:" 2 Peter 1:3

"For this reason we also, since the day we heard it, do not cease to pray for you, and to ask that you may be filled with the knowledge of His will in all wisdom and spiritual understanding; that you may walk worthy of the Lord, fully pleasing *Him,* being fruitful in every good work and increasing in the knowledge of God; strengthened with all might, according to His glorious power, for all patience and longsuffering with joy; giving thanks to the Father who has qualified us to be partakers of the inheritance of the saints in the light." Colossians 1:9-12

...

#44

Help Them Don't Hurt Them!

What if every person with whom you get upset, who irritates you, who drives you crazy, who drives you nuts, who makes you angry, whom you would give anything to turn your back on, who hurts you, who you feel is too needy and obnoxious and annoying and difficult, etc. were an awesome opportunity?

An opportunity to love. An opportunity to forgive. An opportunity to be kind. An opportunity to give. An opportunity to be merciful. An opportunity to be humble. An opportunity to serve. An opportunity to pray for someone. An opportunity to help. An opportunity to do for them whatever the Lord desires. In the name of the Lord for the glory of the Lord. In obedience to God's greatest commands to love Him with all your heart and to love others as yourself. What if?

What if instead of hurting the people who make you feel like tearing your hair out, screaming at the top of your lungs, lashing out at, seeking vengeance toward, being mean to, gossiping about, judging, and condemning, crying out your heart because of, etc., you decided to do what Jesus would do? What the Lord wants you to do?

What if you realized these people need the Lord, need His love, forgiveness, grace, mercy, salvation, provision, and help, and need to see the Lord's love in others? What if you saw each and every one of these people for the rest of your life from this day forward as an opportunity to obey God's greatest commands?

Let us not miss our opportunities, friend. Let us humble ourselves before God almighty, repent of any sinful thoughts, feelings, words, and actions, and choose to seek and follow the Lord in how He leads us to love and serve others in His name. For His glory, oh yes!

"Love does no harm to a neighbor; therefore love *is* the fulfillment of the law." Romans 13:10 NKJV

"Owe no one anything except to love one another, for he who loves another has fulfilled the law." Romans 13:8 NKJV

…

#45

God Saved My Life Today

I was driving down the highway with my special needs ministry dogs in a relatively small town when seemingly out of nowhere a car started driving across the highway at a slow speed whereby it was obvious I would end up crashing into it due to the car being perpendicular to me and not getting out of my way nearly fast enough.

Additionally, the traffic behind me would inevitably crash into me. In all honesty, due to all the factors involved, I do not believe it was humanly and physically possible that I could have done anything other than crash really hard into the car and likely become part of a multi-car accident. I am 100% certain that God almighty reached down His heavenly hand and saved my life. I not only didn't crash. I didn't have to slam on my breaks. I didn't get injured. The dogs didn't get thrown forward in the car. It was seriously as though the Lord simply rearranged everything to save my life as well as the lives of the others. But this message isn't about how beyond-description thankful to the Lord I am. It's about this.

I reflected after I drove on in utter awe and thanksgiving to God how I no longer want God to protect me and save my life so I can go on living for me seeking personal happiness, worldly pleasures, and the fulfillment of self-centered dreams. I literally want to spend every breath of my remaining time on this earth loving and serving and worshiping and praising and glorifying the Lord with every single ounce of my heart as I strive daily to fulfill my life's calling. To be a totally devoted follower of the Lord Jesus Christ and to help others to become and remain totally devoted followers of the Lord Jesus Christ.

Today God saved my life. And I yearn more than ever before to bring Him praise, honor, and glory forever and to help others to do the same!

Oh, yes, He saved my life. For His glory, Hallelujah! Amen!

I feel compelled to ask you this, friend. It shouldn't take a miraculous experience like I had today for us to consider this question. For the rest of your time on this earth, and forever, is it your greatest desire to bring love, praise, honor, and glory to the Lord God almighty? Oh, may it be so!

"who has saved us and called *us* with a holy calling, not according to our works, but according to His own purpose and grace which was given to us in Christ Jesus before time began," 2 Timothy 1:9

"For by grace you have been saved through faith, and that not of yourselves; *it is* the gift of God, not of works, lest anyone should boast. For we are His workmanship, created in Christ Jesus for good works, which God prepared beforehand that we should walk in them." Ephesians 2:8-10

"and He died for all, that those who live should live no longer for themselves, but for Him who died for them and rose again." 2 Corinthians 5:15

...

#46

Why Are You Crying?

"Why are you crying?" I heard the Holy Spirit speak quietly to my heart.

I was right on the cusp of crying. The tears were edging up to my eyes as I prepared to cry. Something I did very little of in recent years. Something I find myself doing seemingly daily now [when I wrote the message for a short season].

Why would God ask me that question when He already knew? I believe this. That He wanted to remind me that He is the "God of all comfort", that it is okay to cry, and that He as my heavenly Father is lovingly there for me when I as His daughter and servant cry.

I've been crying because of the cruelty of people toward me which has been increasing as so much of this world has its back turned to the Lord. I've been crying because I've had so very much loss in my life. I've been crying over others' sorrows, trials, and tribulations. And, most of all, I've been crying as I pray for people all around the world as I stand in the gap for a world in dire need of the Lord Jesus Christ.

I believe God wanted to remind me I do not cry alone. He is God Emmanuel. God who is with His children. God who will comfort and heal the hurting hearts of those who turn unto Him.

Do you ever cry? Turn, turn, turn to the Lord. Do not cry alone, friend. Cry your tears before the Lord. In His presence find the comfort only He can give. Amen!

"Blessed *be* the God and Father of our Lord Jesus Christ, the Father of mercies and God of all comfort, who comforts us in all our tribulation, that we may be able to comfort those who are in any trouble, with the comfort with which we ourselves are comforted by God. For as the sufferings of Christ abound in us, so our consolation also abounds through Christ." 2 Corinthians 1:3-5 NKJV

...

#47

God Help the People Hurting Me

"God please help the people hurting me," I prayed.

God has so amazingly, blessedly, mercifully, and miraculously been transforming me over the years. I don't want to hurt those who hurt me as I once did. I don't want vengeance. I don't want to feel sorry for myself. I don't want to hold onto hurt and bitterness. I don't want to gossip and slander them. I want to forgive them. And, more than anything, I want to love them, bless them, do good to them, and pray for them as Jesus tells us to do. And I want to repent when I fall short in all this. I want to love the way God commands us to love.

I have always been very sensitive, and I get worn out by seemingly how often people hurt me these days. With the world falling apart, with less and less love and more and more evil on this earth, and given my exceeding love for and devotion to the Lord and my calling as an evangelist on the road for Jesus, I am at pretty high risk of being treated badly.

But God amazingly is teaching me how to deny self, take up my cross, follow Him, and to love the very people who are hurting me. I find myself desperate now that those who hurt me know the love of God, turn to Jesus Christ as Lord, have a forever relationship with God instead of spending eternity in hell and the lake of fire apart from Him, have their needs met on this earth, fulfill the Lord's will for their lives, and above all else become and remain totally devoted followers of the Lord Jesus Christ. I want them to enjoy the love of Jesus for eternity and to love and worship and praise and honor and glorify God forevermore.

Sure, it's really hard to be hurt. I cry sometimes over how people treat me. But I have learned to bring my tears, heart, and hurt to the Lord for healing and comfort and to cry out to the Lord in prayer for those who hurt me. And to love and help and bless them with the love of God.

Friend, with all my heart, I beg you to do this. Humble yourself, bring any hurt to the Lord for healing and comfort, repent of any sin in your heart, words, and mouth, forgive the people who hurt you, and love them with the love of Jesus, bless them, do good to them, and pray for them. This, friend, is the way of the Lord. The way we are called to live. For the glory of Christ, yes it is!

"Then He said to *them* all, "If anyone desires to come after Me, let him deny himself, and take up his cross daily, and follow Me." Luke 9:23

"You have heard that it was said, 'YOU SHALL LOVE YOUR NEIGHBOR and hate your enemy.' But I say to you, love your enemies, bless those who curse you, do good to those who hate you, and pray for those who spitefully use you and persecute you, that you may be sons of your Father in heaven; for He makes His sun rise on the evil and on the good, and sends rain on the just and on the unjust." Matthew 5:43-45 NKJV

. . .

#48

Thank You for Leading Me to Repentance

"Thank you for leading me to repentance," I told the Lord.

I had been going through quite a fiery trial concerning a certain situation and the really tough and challenging way some people had been treating me, but I have long since learned other people's wrongdoing and their need to be held accountable by the Lord does not justify our not taking responsibility for our own sin and repenting.

Not only did the Lord blessedly give me love and forgiveness for those people, but He lovingly and mercifully albeit firmly and sternly showed me my own wrongdoing and led me to repentance.

Why would I be thankful? Repentance doesn't feel very good to say the least. The answer is clearly revealed in these verses

"And you have forgotten the exhortation which speaks to you as to sons: "MY SON, DO NOT DESPISE THE CHASTENING OF THE LORD, NOR BE DISCOURAGED WHEN YOU ARE REBUKED BY HIM; FOR WHOM THE LORD LOVES HE CHASTENS, AND SCOURGES EVERY SON WHOM HE RECEIVES." If you endure chastening, God deals with you as with sons; for what son is there whom a father does not chasten? But if you are without chastening, of which all have become partakers, then you are illegitimate and not sons. Furthermore, we have had human fathers who corrected *us,* and we paid *them* respect. Shall we not much more readily be in subjection to the Father of spirits and live? For they indeed for a few days chastened *us* as seemed *best* to them, but He for *our* profit, that *we* may be partakers of His holiness. Now no chastening seems to be joyful for the present, but painful; nevertheless, afterward it yields the peaceable fruit of righteousness to those who have been trained by it." Hebrews 12:5-11 NKJV

...

#49

The Lady who Hates Me

I know a lady who hates me. I have never done anything to hurt her. I have gone out of my way to be kind and loving toward her, to engage her in conversation, to show her care, to express interest in her life, to encourage her, to give a little gift to her. Why does she hate me, how does she show her hatred, how did I handle people's hatred and wrongdoing in the past, how do I handle it now, and how should you handle it when it comes your way?

I believe she hates me because my following Jesus likely makes her question her lifestyle not following Him, and I have brought to light some things that created some work for her she didn't want to do. She shows her hatred with coldness, meanness, rudeness, lashing out, and probably gossip. In the past I handled people's wrongdoing with hatred, manipulation, control, lashing out, judgment, criticism, condemnation, pride, vengeance, trying to hurt those hurting me, feeling sorry for myself, withdrawing at times, etc.

Now I do my best to handle people's hatred and other wrongdoing with LOVE, MERCY, GRACE, FORGIVENESS, KINDNESS, GOODNESS, PRAYING FOR THEM, and bringing my hurt and such to the Lord for love, wisdom, healing, and comfort.

How should you handle people's hatred and wrongdoing? According to the will of God almighty.

Please consider the powerful words of the Lord Jesus Christ:

""Judge not, and you shall not be judged. Condemn not, and you shall not be condemned. Forgive, and you will be forgiven." Luke 6:37

"Repay no one evil for evil. Have regard for good things in the sight of all men. If it is possible, as much as depends on you, live peaceably with all men. Beloved, do not avenge yourselves, but *rather* give place to wrath; for it is written, "VENGEANCE IS MINE, I WILL REPAY," says the Lord. Therefore "IF YOUR ENEMY IS HUNGRY, FEED HIM; IF HE IS THIRSTY, GIVE HIM A DRINK; FOR IN SO DOING YOU WILL HEAP COALS OF FIRE ON HIS HEAD." Do not be overcome by evil, but overcome evil with good." Romans 12:17-21 NKJV

"You have heard that it was said, 'YOU SHALL LOVE YOUR NEIGHBOR and hate your enemy.' But I say to you, love your enemies, bless those who curse you, do good to those who hate you, and pray for those who spitefully use you and persecute you, that you may be sons of your Father in heaven; for He makes His sun rise on the evil and on the good, and sends rain on the just and on the unjust. Matthew 5:43-45 NKJV

…

#50

This Is NOT Letting Go

When God makes clear He wants us to let go of someone or something, and we break ties physically but go on with our lives continually thinking about that person or thing, I believe this is NOT the extent of the letting go God desires.

Nowhere in the Bible can I recall the Lord telling His people to think continually about whom and what He tells them to let go. I can't think of any instance in which God tells His followers to focus their hearts and minds on the past and to keep their focus there.

Rather, God makes ultra clear He is to be our first love (Rev. 2:4-5), we are to have no gods before Him (Exodus 20:3), He is the one we are to worship and nothing and nobody else (Matthew 4:10), He is to be preeminent in our lives (Colossians 1:18), we are to keep our minds "stayed" on Him (Isaiah 26:3), we are to focus our minds on things above (Colossians 3:2), we are to meditate on His Word throughout the day and night (Joshua 1:8), and the following is to be a guideline for what we think about in general:

"Finally, brethren, whatever things are true, whatever things *are* noble, whatever things *are* just, whatever things *are* pure, whatever things *are* lovely, whatever things *are* of good report, if *there is* any virtue and if *there is* anything praiseworthy—meditate on these things." Philippians 4:8 NKJV

God's greatest command is to love Him with all our hearts, minds, souls, and strength (Mark 12:30). If we are thinking constantly about anything or anyone He told us to let go, we need to stop and turn our focus to the Lord, to His Word, and to His will for us each and every day going forth.

Need to do some letting go?

...

#51

When God Says NO to What You Want

This very morning that I write this message, just minutes ago in fact, God made clear for the second time that what I wanted to do today is NOT His will. In effect, He said NO. Immediately I was at a crossroads. Which way would I go? I believe every time God says NO to something we want and makes known what His will is instead, we stand at a crossroads.

The most obvious aspect of the crossroads is that we need to decide to do God's will in loving obedience to Him – or rebel against Him and go our own way.

But this is not all. We also need to decide when we choose to humble ourselves and to do His will whether we will do so with OUR HEARTS, OUR WORDS, AND OUR ACTIONS honoring and glorifying to Him – or not.

Will we feel sorry for ourselves, throw a temper tantrum, fall into a depression, get angry at God, follow Him like a two-year-old child dragging our feet, sucking our thumbs, and complaining? Or will we follow Him with genuine love and devotion and make known to Him that it is our honor, privilege, and a blessing to faithfully follow Him wherever He leads us?

Today, in the strength of the Lord Jesus Christ for the glory of the Lord Jesus Christ, I purpose it in my heart to follow the Lord with love, joy, and thanksgiving – and to repent when I fall short. Far too many times over the years, I have done anything but. I either rebelled against Him altogether. Or I followed Him with a bad, self-pitying attitude.

Now, at long last, I am totally devoted to the Lord Jesus Christ, and I hunger and thirst for righteousness. And I am satisfied and fulfilled not in getting everything I want but in being given the unfathomably wonderful privilege of enjoying a deeply intimate, ever-growing personal relationship with the Lord that comes with a lifestyle of total devotion to Him. A lifestyle of obedience with love, humility, joy, thanksgiving, and repentance when needed is an instrumental part of having such a beautiful, rich, and vibrant intimate relationship with Jesus.

Which way will you go, friend, when you stand at that crossroads? Please choose the right way. God's way. Obey Him with the right heart. Get rid of any self-pity, complaining, arguing, anger, bitterness, hurt, pride, etc. Follow Jesus with the right heart! Praise the Lord! AMEN!

"Blessed are those who hunger and thirst for righteousness, For they shall be filled." Matthew 5:6 NKJV

...

#52

My Mother Was Right

Shortly after I started some physical therapy, the therapist made clear I needed to learn to have better posture and put my shoulders back. Would you believe DECADES ago my Mom used to take me clothes shopping and tell me in the dressing room to PUT MY SHOULDERS BACK? Stubborn, prideful, rebellious, lazy, and foolish, I refused. My mother was right.

May seem funny on the surface as we tend to joke about the rebellion of teenagers. But it's actually tragic how throughout our lives no matter our ages we can be stubborn, prideful, rebellious, lazy, and foolish. We can be this way with God, and we can be this way with the people God uses to give us help, support, wisdom, and direction. It is all SIN we need to get rid of.

Some if not many of us need to get our acts together and repent and start humbling ourselves before God and others and live in obedience to God - and leave the sin behind. Amen!

"A man's pride will bring him low, But the humble in spirit will retain honor." Proverbs 29:23

"Pride *goes* before destruction, And a haughty spirit before a fall." Proverbs 16:18

"The fear of the LORD *is* to hate evil; Pride and arrogance and the evil way And the perverse mouth I hate." Proverbs 8:13

…

#53

Please Do Not Do This!

"This is an action I do not want you to take," the Holy Spirit spoke to my heart as I headed in the direction of doing something I felt strongly I must do.

The Lord stopped me in my tracks. I turned in another direction. Once upon a time I would have pridefully marched on in the direction I wanted to go. See, I used to live for me. But the Lord shows us in the Bible His followers aren't to live for self anymore. We are to live for Him. He has transformed me beyond belief and continues to transform me day by day and is so merciful as I learn to walk with Him and repent when necessary.

Too many, I am afraid, call Jesus Lord and call themselves Christians but live for self not for Jesus. This is exactly what I did until the Lord set me straight.

I really wanted to take that action. I truly felt it was best. And oh how the lust of my flesh would have been satisfied! But I no longer live to satisfy self. I live to love and serve and satisfy and worship and glorify the Lord!

Friend, if there is something you're thinking about doing, or something you have already begun, and it is not the will of God, please don't do it. Please deny self, take up your cross, and follow the Lord down the pathway of righteousness He sets before you! Amen!

"and He died for all, that those who live should live no longer for themselves, but for Him who died for them and rose again." 2 Cor. 5:15 NKJV

"When He had called the people to *Himself,* with His disciples also, He said to them, "Whoever desires to come after Me, let him deny himself, and take up his cross, and follow Me." Mark 8:34 NKVJ

"…He leads me in the paths of righteousness For His name's sake." Psalms 23:3 NKJV

…

#54

God Knows What He's Doing

God knows what He's doing. Of course He does. He is God. He is Lord. He is Savior. He is holy. He is all knowing. He is all wise. He is all powerful. He is sovereign. He is Creator of the universe. And on and on His attributes and character and awesomeness and amazingness go. So why am I telling you God knows what He's doing when it's so totally obvious?

BECAUSE SOMETIMES WE THINK AND FEEL AND ACT LIKE GOD DOESN'T KNOW WHAT HE'S DOING. Sometimes in our humanness, in our flesh, in our sinfulness, in our pride and fear and anxiety and doubt and worry and self-righteousness and anger and any other manner of wrongfulness, we foolishly believe God doesn't know what He's doing. And we think, feel, and act like He doesn't. Which is very bad, very wrong, and very dangerous.

The truth is God ALWAYS knows what He's doing. If we are thinking, feeling, or acting like He doesn't, let us HUMBLE OURSELVES,

REPENT, PURIFY OURSELVES, PUT OUR TRUST IN HIM, SEEK HIM, HEAR HIM, OBEY HIM, LIVE FOR HIM, and LOVE, PRAISE, HONOR, ADORE, WORSHIP, SERVE, and GLORIFY HIM! Forever!

"Trust in the LORD with all your heart, And lean not on your own understanding; In all your ways acknowledge Him, And He shall direct your paths." Proverbs 3:5-6 NKJV

...

#55

Cry Your Tears to God

I learned at a young age tears were bad. Crying was discouraged. It was not a good thing to do. I was essentially told I was too sensitive, too emotional, too dramatic. I realized it would be best to hide my crying or face the consequences. Of being looked down upon, judged, criticized, considered strange and different, laughed at. My dear beloved parents probably didn't know better. They had likely been raised to not cry or to hide their tears. In over ½ century of my life, I can likely count on one hand how many times I have seen a tear or two in either of my parents' eyes. Letting ourselves cry, and knowing what to do with those tears, no matter the reason, it's not so easy for some of us. I am so thankful God has taught me what to do with my tears.

From the little I recall of my young years, I am sure I cried a good bit. For decades as a younger adult, I cried in my utter brokenness. In recent years, I cried relatively little. Now, recently, I have started crying once more. This time around, I know what to do with my tears.

I come into the presence of the Lord, commune with Him, pour out my whole heart to Him, cry before Him, give Him my tears, share my thoughts and feelings with Him, pray to Him, seek Him, open the Bible which I read daily, and sometimes come to Him without the Bible open but with my heart wide open to Him. And I find love, mercy, grace, peace, joy, wisdom, forgiveness, rest, comfort, kindness, care, compassion, gentleness, tenderness, protection, refuge, restoration, refreshing, fellowship, friendship, direction, healing, hope, shelter, and gigantic wings to hide beneath – in Him. Yes, day by day I am learning what it means to truly abide in Christ. To put my trust and expectation in Him and my heart and life in His blessed everlasting loving hands. Tears and all.

Now my eyes tear up as I finish this message. How thankful I am to know my tears are not wasted. God sees them. And now God is using the love, sensitivity, compassion, and tears He has given me to help others to know the very best and most precious place to come with our tears is into the glorious presence of God almighty through the Lord Jesus Christ, AMEN!

"From the end of the earth I will cry to You, When my heart is overwhelmed; Lead me to the rock that is higher than I. For You have been a shelter for me, A strong tower from the enemy. I will abide in Your tabernacle forever; I will trust in the shelter of Your wings. Selah."" Psalms 61:2-4 NKJV

"Trust in Him at all times, you people; Pour out your heart before Him; God *is* a refuge for us. Selah" Psalms 62:8 NKJV

…

#56

A Quiet Place of Rest

After some years on the road for Jesus full-time with my special needs ministry dogs, given the extreme challenge and exhaustion of it all, I truly looked forward to returning to a previous location I was confident after much praying would be "a quiet place of rest". Given the location, climate, culture, familiarity of the area, and the beach I and paralyzed ministry dog Miss Mercy adore, surely I would enjoy my "quiet place of rest" where I could rest, write, seek the Lord for direction going forward, and do a little bit of ministry work. To my total surprise – and utter dismay – my "quiet place of rest" despite some beautiful blessings turned out to be ultra challenging and exceedingly uncomfortable for reasons I won't go into.

What happened to the "quiet place of rest" to which I had fully believed God had led me? I genuinely believed God had spoken to my heart a promise that I would have "a quiet place of rest". But this was anything but!

The Lord wanted to teach me a powerful lesson. He wanted me to learn how to do something I have needed to learn for a very long time. The "quiet place of rest" for Jesus' followers is to be first and foremost IN CHRIST. Is to be above all else IN ABIDING IN JESUS. Such that no matter how much chaos, storm, trials, tribulations, challenges, noise, battles, craziness, etc. there may be around us, we can ABIDE IN THE LORD. We can have "a quiet place of rest" in THE LORD and in a PERSONAL FOREVER RELATIONSHIP WITH HIM and in INTIMATE FELLOWSHIP IN HIS GLORIOUS PRESENCE.

Simply put, no matter what goes on around us, we can choose to trust in the Lord, to put our faith in Him, to depend on Him, to hope in Him, to put our expectation in Him, to commune with Him, to spend time alone in His presence, to rejoice in Him, to find joy in Him, to rest in Him, to find peace in Him, to praise and adore Him, to worship Him, to love Him, to experience and enjoy His love for us, to find wisdom, direction, counsel, and comfort in Him, to find healing, restoration, refreshing, rejuvenation, and revival in Him, to look to Him as Lord, Savior, master, and very best friend, to grow in Him, to be transformed by Him, to draw ever nearer to Him, and Him to us, to grow ever deeper in relationship with Him, oh, yes - and more!

The perfect "quiet place of rest" is not in our circumstances, not in our physical location, not in our relationships with people, not in family and friends, not in our dreams coming to pass, not in anything of this world at all. Oh, sure, we can find wonderful blessings from God in any and all of this when He desires. But it is all temporary and imperfect.

Our perfect, 100% guaranteed, satisfying beyond measure, exhilarating and exciting and blessed "quiet place of rest" is for His followers IN THE LORD JESUS CHRIST – now and forevermore, AMEN!

"Come to Me, all you who labor and are heavy laden, and I will give you rest. Take My yoke upon you and learn from Me, for I am gentle and lowly in heart, and you will find rest for your souls. For My yoke is easy and My burden is light."" Matthew 11:28-30 NKJV

…

#57

Don't Leave Because of Fear

I started thinking seriously about leaving somewhere and something and some people whereby there would have been a major change in my life and ministry. The Holy Spirit spoke strongly to my heart, "Don't leave because of fear."

God wanted me to stay where I was for the time being anyway. He didn't want me to yield to the fear and run. He wanted me to yield and surrender to Him and stay where He wanted me. To do what He wanted me to do and so He could teach me something and to refine and purify me. He had a plan and purpose for me where I was and wanted me to stay until I had fulfilled His purpose for me there. But I was afraid and uncomfortable and was tempted to run. I stayed. Because Jesus Christ is LORD.

I have a long history of fear, worry, doubt, and anxiety. All sin needing to be gotten rid of. God is continually working on me to live by faith not by fear. I am learning to put my trust in the Lord day by day and to follow Jesus not follow fear.

Just because fear comes doesn't mean we have to let it rule and reign in our hearts and lives. God is the one who is to rule and reign. Fear is not to be our god. The Lord is God.

When we find ourselves afraid, worrying, and anxious, we need to turn away from all of it, turn to the Lord, put our trust in Him, seek Him, hear Him, and lovingly and faithfully obey Him.

This means when our flesh wants to run away in fear, and God wants us to stay, we need to remain where we are unless or until God says it's time to move on.

The right reason to leave somewhere, something, or someone is not because of fear or any other emotion but because it is the will of God.

If you're tempted to run right now out of fear, don't bow down to the fear and run. Seek the Lord, wait on Him, hear Him, and obey Him.

Whether He leads you to stay or go, obey. For He is God – forever and ever, He is Lord, AMEN!

Feeling afraid? PRAY – and love & follow the Lord!

"Be anxious for nothing, but in everything by prayer and supplication, with thanksgiving, let your requests be made known to God; and the peace of God, which surpasses all understanding, will guard your hearts and minds through Christ Jesus." Philippians 4:6-7 NKJV

...

#58

I Don't Want to Stay But –

Sometimes God leads us to stay somewhere, or with someone, or in some situation, or in something, etc., when we feel desperate to get out of where we are, what we're in, whom we're with, etc. We want to do anything but remain. We want out – now. Because we're afraid, uncomfortable, tempted elsewhere or to something or someone else, overwhelmed, unhappy, hurt, angry, wanting something or someone we feel is better, craving change, bored, restless, whatever. Bottom line, we want to go and get away from our current circumstances. Sometimes we desperately don't want to stay, but –

But Jesus Christ is Lord, and we were not created to live for self to love and please self. We were created for God, to experience and enjoy forever fellowship with Him through the Lord Jesus Christ, and to live for Him to love and please Him.

I have always been restless. And I have faced seemingly relentless challenges in my life. I can't tell you how often I have wanted to get away from wherever I am. I used to run. And run and run. Anytime I wanted to go, I went.

Now I see the truth. Jesus' followers belong to Jesus. Jesus' followers aren't to follow the flesh, the world, or the devil. Jesus' followers are to follow Jesus. When God wants us to go, we are to go. When He wants us to stay, we are to stay.

I don't want to stay, but - . Even when our flesh doesn't want to stay, and we are tempted to go, we should remain right where God wants us. We are commanded to love Him with all our hearts. I don't want to stay, but - . Those who love the Lord are to obey the Lord. I don't want to stay, but - . If God is calling you to stay somewhere, or with someone, or in some situation, etc., love the Lord. Obey the Lord. Stay. Not for your sake. Deny self. Take up your cross. Stay. For Christ's sake.

I don't want to stay, but - . Those of us who believe in Jesus Christ as Lord, let us remember God is with us. When He tells us to stay, and we obey, we are not there where He desires we be by ourselves. God is with us. And in Him, through Him, for Him, we will find the love, strength, grace, mercy, wisdom, power, etc. to be where He wants us to be. For Christ's sake, when He says stay, let us stay! Amen!

"If anyone serves Me, let him follow Me; and where I am, there My servant will be also. If anyone serves Me, him *My* Father will honor." John 12:26 NKJV

"Then He said to *them* all, "If anyone desires to come after Me, let him deny himself, and take up his cross daily, and follow Me. For whoever desires to save his life will lose it, but whoever loses his life for My sake will save it." Luke 9:23-24 NKJV

...

#59

When God Says Do Something

"When I say do something, do it," the Holy Spirit spoke to my heart.

May seem totally obvious, but some of us need to hear it, don't we? I know I do. I believe there is always more growth for me to do in terms of obedience to God. Of humbly and submissively obeying the Lord in all things without debate, resistance, arguing, questioning, or outright rebellion. Of simply praying for and discerning God's will – and doing whatever He tells me to do.

Good, loving parents teach their children that when they tell their children to do something, their children need to do it. How much more so should God's children obey the Lord in whatever He gives us to do.

Is there something the Lord has been speaking to your heart to do? Something He has brought to light in the Bible you need to do that you haven't been doing?

If there is something God is telling you to do, do it!

" "I WILL BE A FATHER TO YOU, AND YOU SHALL BE MY SONS AND DAUGHTERS, SAYS THE LORD ALMIGHTY." " 2 Cor. 6:18 NKJV

…

#60

When God Says STAY OUT OF IT!

God's words to me were very clear. "Stay out of it!" His Holy Spirit spoke strongly to my heart. Let me tell you, it wasn't the first time God had instructed me not to jump into a certain situation that was filled with trouble, drama, evil, and major distraction. At times, He had led me to pray. He had even led me to help with the situation in a limited way. But I had gone beyond the limit the Lord had set for me. I had repented. Now I was on the verge of getting involved again without the Holy Spirit leading me to do so. Thus the strong warning.

I have a very strong sense God is compelling me to write this message because some if not many who read it need to hear these exact words. Stay out of it!

Friend, is there any area of your life in which the Lord is warning you to stay out of something? Or to stay out of someone's life? To not get involved? Or even to step back from something or someone with which or with whom you've already gotten involved? Do you sense He wants you to stay out of it and pray from the sidelines while God deals with the situation and person/people? Or do you sense He wants you to not be distracted by whatever or whomever it is and to turn in a different direction to serve Him elsewhere? Or do you sense He wants you to spend the time you would have used being involved to be with Him instead praying, studying the Bible, and praising, worshiping, and singing to Him?

If you are clear through prayer and reading the Bible and having a strong relationship with the Lord and seeking godly counsel if/when/as the Lord leads you that God is telling you to stay out of it, you know what to do. STAY OUT OF IT!

"How much better *is it* to get wisdom than gold! and to get understanding rather to be chosen than silver!" Proverbs 16:16 NKJV

"For wisdom is better than rubies; and all the things that may be desired are not to be compared to it." Proverbs 8:11 NKJV

Let us pray for wisdom - and obey the Lord!

…

#61

When Friends Let You Down

When friends let you down, what should you do? I have been on both sides of the fence. I have let friends down, and I have been let down by friends. Let's face it. We're all imperfect. And friendships aren't always easy. And people not just others but ourselves included can present challenges. But if we're committed followers of Jesus, over time we should be letting friends down less. And we should be handling things better when friends let us down. What exactly should we do when friend let us down?

The obvious per the Bible is we should love them, forgive them, pray for them, bless them, do good to them, be merciful with them, be kind to them, etc. We should repent before God of any of our own wrongdoing and seek their forgiveness if and as the Lord leads us. And we should pray and seek God's will concerning if He wants us to make any changes regarding the friendship such as if He wants us to remain friends, to spend more or less time together, to treat our friends differently, to listen more, to give more, to encourage more, to take a season apart from our friends, to let go of the friendship because He is leading us elsewhere or because the friendship is not ordained by Him, etc.

But this message is not about any of that. Instead I am compelled to share with you an exceedingly beautiful blessing I have found when it comes to friends letting us down or regarding anything sad, painful, hurtful, discouraging, burdensome, challenging, etc. in life for that matter. And herein is the wisdom God has given me.

Come to Jesus. Place your full trust in Him. Come into the shelter of God almighty. Bring your hurting heart and all your thoughts and feelings to Him. Pour out your heart to Him. Come into His refuge. Come under His wings. Rest in His shelter. Fall down before Him. Lie prostrate before Him. Or get on your knees and pray to Him. Or curl up on your bed and seek and receive His comfort. Draw closer to Him. Open the Bible. Bask in the treasures within. Seek wisdom from God. Find healing in Jesus. Commune with the Lord. Rejoice in Jesus.

Find peace and hope in God. Bring your expectation to Him who will never let you down. Give God your tears. Enjoy His company. Experience His presence. Be still. In Him and in His love find all you need. Be restored by Him. Be refreshed and renewed. Draw ever closer to Him and Him to you. Experience His lovingkindness, His tenderness. Find safety in Him. Let Him be your defense. Your fortress. Hide in Him. Bask in His light. Abide. Yes, abide in the Lord Jesus Christ.

There is one Lord. One God. One Savior. One Father in heaven (Ephesians 4:4-6). May He be your Lord, God, Savior, Father, healer, comforter, first love, and your very best friend FOREVER. Rejoice, rejoice, rejoice, oh rejoice! Rejoice, rejoice, rejoice, oh rejoice!

Over the years, many times I have found beautiful, powerful, healing, encouraging, comforting verses on God being a refuge, shelter, fortress, watchtower, defense, secret place, hiding place, safety, etc. for His people. I encourage you to seek and find them in the Bible and to be inspired and moved by them to abide in the Lord! Oh, abide!

"A man *who has* friends must himself be friendly, But there is a friend *who* sticks closer than a brother." Proverbs 18:24 NKJV

"For You have been a shelter for me, A strong tower from the enemy." Psalms 61:3 NKJV

"I will abide in Your tabernacle forever; I will trust in the shelter of Your wings..." Psalms 61:4 NKJV

"He who dwells in the secret place of the Most High Shall abide under the shadow of the Almighty. I will say of the LORD, "*He is* my refuge and my fortress; My God, in Him I will trust."" Psalms 91:1-2 NKJV

"Trust in Him at all times, you people; Pour out your heart before Him; God *is* a refuge for us..." Psalms 62:8 NKJV

...

#62

Anything or Anyone You Need to Leave Behind?

When Jesus called two sets of brothers to come follow Him, they didn't hesitate to follow Him immediately. Not only was their obedience immediate, but it came with a cost. They had to leave much behind in order to follow Him, and the verses below probably reveal just a tiny bit of what they had to leave behind in the way of the familiar, what was comfortable, their work, possessions, friends, family members, where they lived, etc. When faced with following Jesus or holding onto all they had and knew, they chose Jesus and were willing to pay the price of leaving it all behind.

I am compelled to ask you this. Are there any people, places, things, beliefs, habits, addictions, wishes, ways, wants, dreams, attitudes, ways of treating people, anything or anyone at all the Lord has made clear you need to leave behind and that you are refusing to let go in order to fully, freely, and faithfully follow Jesus?

I encourage you to pray, to seek the Lord, to read the Bible, to wait on the Lord, to hear Him, to trust Him, to obey Him, to live to love, serve, and glorify Him, to praise, honor, adore, and worship Him, and to humbly follow Him no matter the cost. No matter what or whom you must leave behind in order to do so. Oh, follow Jesus! Follow Him forth, Hallelujah, AMEN!

"And Jesus, walking by the Sea of Galilee, saw two brothers, Simon called Peter, and Andrew his brother, casting a net into the sea; for they were fishermen. Then He said to them, "Follow Me, and I will make you fishers of men." They immediately left *their* nets and followed Him. Going on from there, He saw two other brothers, James *the son* of Zebedee, and John his brother, in the boat with Zebedee their father, mending their nets. He called them, and immediately they left the boat and their father, and followed Him." Matthew 4:18-22 NKJV

. . . .

#63

Jesus Calling – the Right Way to Respond

When Jesus called four men to follow Him in the Bible verses below, their responses to Jesus's call show us four truths about the right way to respond to Jesus calling.

1. When Jesus is calling, we are to hear the Lord.
2. When Jesus is calling, we are to obey the Lord according to His will for us.

3. When Jesus is calling, we are to obey the Lord according to His timing even when that means He is leading us to act immediately.

4. When Jesus is calling, we are to humbly, submissively, joyfully follow the Lord wherever and however and to whatever and to whomever He leads us with total surrender no matter what or whom we need to forsake and leave behind in order to obey and follow Him.

When we stand before the Lord Jesus Christ and have to give an account of our lives as we all one day will do, let it be said of you and I that these four truths were evident in our hearts and lives in response to Jesus calling!

"And Jesus, walking by the Sea of Galilee, saw two brothers, Simon called Peter, and Andrew his brother, casting a net into the sea; for they were fishermen. Then He said to them, "Follow Me, and I will make you fishers of men." They immediately left *their* nets and followed Him. Going on from there, He saw two other brothers, James *the son* of Zebedee, and John his brother, in the boat with Zebedee their father, mending their nets. He called them, and immediately they left the boat and their father, and followed Him." Matthew 4:18-22 NKJV

...

#64

My Bathroom Light Story

When I stayed in the same hotel room at the same hotel several times while in the area for my ministry work, I never thought twice about the bathroom light. The then hotel manager had been in the room, housekeeping had been in the room, and maintenance had been in the room. Nobody said a thing about the light. Then management changed, and a corporate manager came into my room to help with something. He kindly asked if I minded if he would take care of my bathroom light. How so?

He wanted to clean out the bugs and change the bulbs. I told him it would be fine. I figured he was just one of those people who is very particular about things and likes everything clean, neat, and in order. Oh, how wrong I was!

When he was done, I was shocked at how bright the bathroom light was. In my multiple hotel stays in that room, I had just assumed the bathroom light was fine. Now that the bathroom was filled with bright light, I realized how very dim and dark it had been!

Friend, we are to walk, i.e. live, in the light of the Lord Jesus Christ. We are to follow the light of the world, Jesus. We are to have the light of Christ. We are to shine with and reflect the light of Christ.

Our hearts and lives are to be filled with Jesus' light no matter how dark the world around us may be. When we repent, believe in Jesus as Lord and in His death and resurrection, turning to God and His ways, we are saved, born again spiritually, and promised a forever relationship with the Lord. We come out of darkness and into the light. But if we're not careful, we may find ourselves at times holding onto the dim and dusky and even dark of what we have always known.

God doesn't call us to a life of darkness. He calls us to a life of His magnificent love and breathtaking light.

The Bible is filled with verses on darkness and verses on light. I encourage you to keep your heart and eyes open to them as you read the Bible – and to go forth living blessedly in the wondrousness and splendor of the light of the Lord Jesus Christ!

"Then Jesus spoke to them again, saying, "I am the light of the world. He who follows Me shall not walk in darkness, but have the light of life."" John 8:12

"Let your light so shine before men, that they may see your good works and glorify your Father in heaven." Matthew 5:16 NKJV

"But you *are* a chosen generation, a royal priesthood, a holy nation, His own special people, that you may proclaim the praises of Him who called you out of darkness into His marvelous light;" 1 Peter 2:9 NKJV

…

#65

Don't Let the Devil Do This

Out of seemingly nowhere I heard these words inside my heart, and I am quite sure since they line up with the Bible and given how I was feeling at the time that the Holy Spirit had spoken this strong encouragement.

"Don't let the devil trample all over you," He said. "Trample over him."

Then a few more words came. "Don't listen to his lies," the Holy Spirit told me. "Believe my Truth [i.e. the Bible]."

In his mission to steal, kill, and destroy (John 10:10), the devil goes to any lengths to lie to us, attack us, deceive us, tempt us, distract us, discourage us, get us depressed and downhearted, wreck our relationship with the Lord, get us off track, convince us we can't do what God calls us to do, convince us God doesn't love and care about us, tear us down, make us focus on ourselves instead of on God and others, get us to give up, terrify us, etc.

He will try just about anything to trample us down, and, if we're not careful, we can end up really broken, messed up, unfocused, disheartened, etc.

Know what Jesus tells the disciples? ""Behold, I give you the authority to trample on serpents and scorpions, and over all the power of the enemy, and nothing shall by any means hurt you.""" Luke 10:19 NKJV

And in the well-known Psalms 91, the psalmist writes of this happening for those who put their trust and take refuge in the Lord:

"You shall tread upon the lion and the cobra, The young lion and the serpent you shall trample underfoot." Psalms 91:13 NKJV

I encourage you to spend time in God's presence daily, read the Bible each and every day, and keep a lookout for verses and passages that encourage you to focus on the Lord and how to how to have victory through the Lord Jesus Christ in your life's battles.

"For whatever is born of God overcomes the world. And this is the victory that has overcome the world—our faith." 1 John 5:4 NKJV

Even as I write this, I have been feeling really down, discouraged, very much on my own, and have done much crying out to the Lord. I hope this message is as much of an encouragement to you as it is to me. Let us look to the Lord! And not allow the enemy to trample us down!

...

#66

God Told Me to Feed My Dogs

The title of this message may sound ridiculous, or hilarious, or foolish, but rest assured I have a powerful message to share with you. Just minutes ago, I was crying out to the Lord yet again about where He wants me to go next in my life on the road for Jesus and ministry with my special needs ministry dogs. In my nearly five years on the road for Him, I have had no permanent residence. Not at all easy in this day and age, with evil abounding, given my personal tough history, and considering I am a middle-aged woman on the road alone with Jesus and my dogs. Obviously the Lord would hurry in response to my cries to tell me His will so I would know the future and not have to be afraid, feel unsettled, be uncomfortable, be anxious, etc., right? Wrong!

"Go feed your dogs," the Holy Spirit spoke to my heart.

The powerful message? God hears His children's cries, His will is perfect, He will answer in His perfect timing, we are to put our trust in Him, and He will order our steps as we faithfully follow Him. And as we wait for Him to reveal His will for us with the seemingly really big things, we should humbly, lovingly, reverently follow Him step by step even down to the very smallest of steps as His Holy Spirit leads us down the pathway He sets before us.

I wanted to know my next location so I could have a sense of security and start getting ready to go when it was time. God wanted me to continue to learn to live by faith in Him instead – and go feed my dogs!

Needing a deeper trust in the Lord? I do! And I have asked Him to help me have just that!

"Be anxious for nothing, but in everything by prayer and supplication, with thanksgiving, let your requests be made known to God; and the peace of God, which surpasses all understanding, will guard your hearts and minds through Christ Jesus." Philippians 4:6-7 NKJV

"Behold, God *is* my salvation, I will trust and not be afraid; 'For YAH, the LORD, *is* my strength and song; He also has become my salvation.'" Isaiah 12:2 NKJV

"The steps of a *good* man are ordered by the LORD, And He delights in his way." Psalms 37:23 NKJV

...

#67

I Have So Much to Do!

"I have so much to do! I don't even know where to begin." I can't remember if I thought essentially those words or spoke them aloud. But the message is clear. Totally overwhelmed. Way too much to do. Where would I start? Surely I would get crushed under the weight of it all. I would probably end up running in a million different directions in a virtual panic – and good excitement too. In a flurry of activity, oh, my, where to begin? How to deal with it all?

Ever felt this way? No sooner than those words had come than the right, and perfect, answer came. This reminder I now share with you.

When we're feeling overloaded, overwhelmed, that we have way too much to do, that everything is just too much, that we don't even know where to start, that surely we'll never get it all done, that the mountain in front of is just too big, that we'll never have enough strength, that we're way too small, that we're way too weary, that we'll never make it through it all, etc., we should TURN TO THE LORD!

May this message be an encouragement to all who come upon it to turn from your sins, believe in Jesus Christ as Lord and in His death and resurrection, turn to God and His ways, ask for and be filled with His Holy Spirit, put your trust in Him, pray to Him, cry out to Him, seek Him, read the Bible, spend time in His presence, love Him, adore Him, praise Him, worship Him, cast your cares upon Him, rest in Him, abide in Him, look to Him, put your hope and expectation in Him, rejoice in Him, celebrate Him, listen for the voice of His Spirit speaking to your heart in line with His Word, ask for and receive all you need including forgiveness, grace, strength, and provision, and be thankful for His amazing love and gracious mercy and glorious presence, oh Hallelujah, AMEN!

"Hear my cry, O God; Attend to my prayer. From the end of the earth I will cry to You, When my heart is overwhelmed; Lead me to the rock that is higher than I." Psalms 61:1-2 NKJV

"casting all your care upon Him, for He cares for you." 1 Peter 5:7 NKJV

…

#68

Where Does God Want You to Go?

"Send me wherever you want me to go," I prayed one day.

I never would have prayed such a prayer in my earlier years of believing in the Lord Jesus Christ. Back then, I pridefully and foolishly thought my life belonged to me and God was there to pray to for what I wanted and needed and to help me get through life.

Today, thanks to God lovingly, mercifully, graciously, and patiently transforming me over time, I am a totally devoted follower of the Lord Jesus Christ. I no longer live for me. I LIVE FOR JESUS my precious and beloved Lord, Savior, master, healer, redeemer, deliverer, teacher, and best friend.

So when it comes to where I go, whether in a given day or in the bigger scheme of things like when God wants me to go to my next location in my life on the road full-time for Jesus and ministry with my special needs ministry dogs, I don't want to make decisions based on my selfish, self-seeking, self-centered, I-want-to-please-me flesh. I want to seek and hear and follow the leading of the Lord. I want to be filled with, led by, and empowered by the Holy Spirit of God who lives in His followers.

Not always easy. Sometimes enormously challenging and hard. But always best and beautiful and most rewarding when I seek where God wants to send me and go where He leads me. Oh, in my exceeding love and passion for the Lord how I yearn to be faithful in this!

Please live for God, friend, not for self. Please don't live according to your own self-centered wishes, ways, and wants that don't line up with God's ways and His will for you. Please forsake all for the Lord He calls you to let go, be totally devoted to Him, and seek and go where He sends you. Today, this very day, and forevermore, AMEN!

Don't know where God wants you to go? PRAY! Know where God wants you to go? Humble yourself! Love Him! Obey Him! Follow Him! Not in your weakness! IN HIS STRENGTH!

"and He died for all, that those who live should live no longer for themselves, but for Him who died for them and rose again." 2 Corinthians 5:15 NKJV

"O LORD, I know the way of man *is* not in himself; *It is* not in man who walks to direct his own steps." Jeremiah 10:23 NKJV

"For you were bought at a price; therefore glorify God in your body and in your spirit, which are God's." 1 Corinthians 6:20 NKJV

…

#69

Don't Jump – WAIT

Ever been so excited, anxious, prideful, eager, desperate, frantic, impatient, angry, irritated, hurting, feeling responsible, in need of something, or anything else for that matter that you have made a rash and impulsive decision and jumped right into something believing that you simply have to get something done NOW before another minute goes by? Only to find that maybe it wasn't such a good idea after all that you jumped in and didn't wait?

I encourage you with all my heart NOT to jump but instead to WAIT. Wait? Yes, wait.

First, as we all should do regularly, purge yourself of any sin. Purify yourself before God. Humbly seek and receive His forgiveness for any sin in your heart, mouth, and actions.

Then, instead of jumping to take action apart from God and His will for you, I encourage you with all my heart to do this.

Pray to the Lord, seek the Lord, WAIT on the Lord, hear the Lord as He speaks to your heart through the Bible and by His Holy Spirit in line with the Bible and through His children if/as He leads you to get godly counsel. Then, when you are clear God has revealed His will to you, in His time, in His strength, according to His ways, with His wisdom, with His love, by His grace and mercy, at His Holy Spirit's leading, for His glory, take action.

Don't jump. Wait. Wait on the Lord. Cry out to Him and trust Him to answer and to lead you forth!

"The LORD *is* good to those who wait for Him, To the soul *who* seeks Him." Lamentations 3:25 NKJV

Pray to God for His will. Pray to God for His wisdom. Pray, pray, pray! Amen! And, of course, OBEY!

"How much better to get wisdom than gold! And to get understanding is to be chosen rather than silver." Proverbs 16:16 NKJV

Please don't live according to the flesh. Live according to the glorious Spirit of almighty God!

...

#70

Time to Call It Quits?

Sometimes we reach a point in our lives in which our circumstances and thoughts and feelings in response to them are such that we wonder if it's time to call it quits with something or someone. Ever felt this way? Feeling that way right now?

Could be a job, career, responsibility, commitment, church, counselor, house, education, friendship, sport, hobby, business, interest, anything or anyone at all.

We may feel exhausted, weary, worn out, burned out, frustrated, impatient, discouraged, down, depressed, anxious, stuck, like we're not getting anywhere and probably never will, like everything is falling apart, like we just can't take it anymore, like surely there are better opportunities and options, etc.

I have experienced this countless times over the years, handled it poorly for years, and am now at long last handling these seasons of my life correctly. Friend, herein is my encouragement to you.

Put your trust in the Lord. Turn to God almighty. Cry out to Him. Pour your heart out to Him. Pray to Him. Seek Him. Wait on Him. Hear Him. Obey Him.

Do not allow your circumstances, thoughts, feelings, other people's opinions, fears, the devil, anything or anyone at all cause you to make a decision about whether or not to call it quits.

Make your decision based on God, the Bible, His will, and His ways. Yield yourself to the Lord and follow Him.

No matter His will, whether He desires you to carry on or to call it quits, seek and trust Him to provide all you need to obey Him.

Pray for wisdom, trust the Lord to give it to you, wait for Him to do so, and love, serve, obey, and glorify God with all your heart! Amen!

"If any of you lacks wisdom, let him ask of God, who gives to all liberally and without reproach, and it will be given to him. But let him ask in faith, with no doubting, for he who doubts is like a wave of the sea driven and tossed by the wind. For let not that man suppose that he will receive anything from the Lord; he is a double-minded man, unstable in all his ways." James 1:5-8 NKJV

…

#71

Hiding from God

The Lord God almighty sees, hears, and knows EVERY single thought, word, and action of all of humanity. Absolutely NOTHING is hidden from Him. Foolishly, unwisely, dangerously, devastatingly, and with great ultimate consequences, sometimes some of us convince ourselves we can hide our sins from God. Oh, sure, we may be able to hide our sins from other people. But never from God.

If you're holding any sin in the dark, I beg you to run to the Lord, cry out to Him with true sorrow over your sin against Him, ask for and receive His forgiveness, and seek all you need from Him to leave the sin behind.

God sent His only Son Jesus Christ to the cross to pay our sin punishment and to raise Him from the dead so all who turn from our sins, believe in Him as Lord and in His death and resurrection, turning to God and His ways, are forgiven, indwelt by the Holy Spirit, promised a forever relationship with God, and are to go forth no longer living for self but to LIVE FOR JESUS in the Lord's most magnificent glorious everlasting light!

"Can anyone hide himself in secret places, So I shall not see him?" says the LORD; "Do I not fill heaven and earth?" says the LORD." Jeremiah 23:24 NKJV

"For there is nothing hidden which will not be revealed, nor has anything been kept secret but that it should come to light." Mark 4:22 NKJV

"And there is no creature hidden from His sight, but all things *are* naked and open to the eyes of Him to whom we *must give* account." Hebrews 4:13 NKJV

"But you *are* a chosen generation, a royal priesthood, a holy nation, His own special people, that you may proclaim the praises of Him who called you out of darkness into His marvelous light;" 1 Peter 2:9 NKJV

"But if we walk in the light as He is in the light, we have fellowship with one another, and the blood of Jesus Christ His Son cleanses us from all sin." 1 John 1:7 NKJV

"and He died for all, that those who live should live no longer for themselves, but for Him who died for them and rose again." 2 Corinthians 5:15 NKJV

…

#72

Why Are You Still Holding On?

If you are clear God wants you to let go of something or someone, why are you still holding on?

Please consider these words from the Lord Jesus Christ.

""But why do you call Me 'Lord, Lord,' and not do the things which I say?" Luke 6:46 NKJV

There are three reasons I had tremendous trouble letting go in the past. First, I didn't believe in God and didn't know His will nor have the strength from God to let go. Second, when I did come to believe in Him, for years I was still living for self not for Him so I didn't have the desperate desire I do now to love, please, honor, and obey Him. Third, once I surrendered and began to truly live for Him I wanted to let go to please Him but was still putting my hope, rest, trust, faith, expectation in myself, people, places, and things and therefore holding on for dear life to all of this instead of abiding in Him and holding onto Him for dear life.

Today, I am a totally devoted follower of the Lord Jesus Christ and with all my heart encourage you to be the same. I no longer cling to this world as I once did. I cleave to the Lord! I hold on for dear life to Him. And when His Holy Spirit brings conviction that I have started once again to hold onto something or someone else, I know I must repent! For the one to hold onto

– ALWAYS – is Jesus! We are to hold onto Jesus as we LIVE FOR JESUS! Hallelujah!

Friend, may we all humble ourselves before God almighty, love, fear, honor, revere, praise, serve, worship, and glorify Him, and in so doing hold onto Him and let go of all He tells us to let go!

"and He died for all, that those who live should live no longer for themselves, but for Him who died for them and rose again." 2 Corinthians 5:15 NKJV

Need wisdom, willingness, and the strength to stop holding on? Need help letting go? Call upon the name of the Lord, Hallelujah, AMEN!

. . .

#73

Feeling Fed Up?

When someone shared with me how fed up he was about a particular situation, I listened, I loved, and I prayed for him with tears. A few minutes after we parted ways, God placed this message on my heart.

About what to do when we're feeling fed up. Like we're at the end of our rope. Like we just can't take it anymore. Like enough is enough. Like the burden is too much. Like we're too worn out to carry on. Like enough of this nonsense. Like if those people don't get their acts together and start doing things right and treating people right, well, you know.

Like no way are we going to continue down that path, how could we be so foolish to do so? Like what in the world are we going to do next when we're ready to scream, cry, tear our hair out, have a meltdown, breakdown, quit on the spot, seek vengeance, lose our minds, well, surely you get the point.

Ever felt this way? I have a zillion times over. Friend, I want to encourage you to do 5 things I have at long last learned to do when I am feeling fed up.

1. Run to the Lord
2. Pour out your heart to the Lord
3. Seek and receive God's forgiveness for any of your thoughts, words, or actions that are sin against God
4. Forgive any and all people you need to forgive
5. Do not act or react until you have prayed to God, sought Him, waited on Him, read and/or meditated on the Bible, heard the Lord speak by His Spirit to your heart which He always does in line with the Bible, and obey the Lord

I had no plans to write this message. I had no idea what I would write. I had no outline. No agenda. I simply knew to write it, knew I had five points to share with you, and all 5 points just poured out of me onto the keyboard until this message was written.

May you be blessed, encouraged, inspired, and challenged in reading this message written from my heart to any and all who have ever, are now, or ever will feel fed up! Hallelujah, AMEN!

"Trust in Him at all times, you people; Pour out your heart before Him; God *is* a refuge for us..." Psalms 62:8 NKJV

...

#74

The Key to Passing God's Tests

After years of desperately wanting to please God but failing miserably in passing so many of the tests He has given me, I was delighted to at long last have a day of sweet victory. The reason for all the years of failure and for that blessed day of victory I share with you now.

I failed time and again for years because I tried to exert myself in my human weakness apart from God as though I needed to prove myself to God and pass His tests without Him.

That day of victory, I called upon the name of the Lord, I prayed, I sought Him, I put my trust in Him not in me, I depended on Him, I abided in Him, I looked to Him, I knew I would fail without Him, I asked for Him to fill me with His Holy Spirit once again, I followed the leading of His Spirit, and I relied on the love, power, mercy, grace, and strength of His Spirit living inside me.

I was victorious THROUGH THE LORD JESUS CHRIST. I denied self, died to self, took up my cross, and followed the Lord (Luke 9:23). I yielded myself to Jesus that He would live through me (Galatians 2:20). I lived for God not for me (2 Cor. 5:15). We are to LIVE FOR JESUS! I lived according to His ways not the world's as I learn studying the Bible every day. Which means I loved when I would have hated. I forgave when I would have sought vengeance. I chose mercy not bitterness. I chose His will not mine. I chose to be thankful even though my flesh was really uncomfortable with my circumstances. And I take no glory for any of this. ALL glory belongs to the Lord! Absolutely ALL the glory is HIS!

How foolish it is when we think we can follow Jesus without Jesus. How foolish it is when we think we can pass God's tests without the Spirit of God. How foolish it is when we trust in our flesh rather than in the Lord and His power and all else He supplies us.

Oh, what blessed victory we can have when we turn, turn, turn to the Lord!

"Are you so foolish? Having begun in the Spirit, are you now being made perfect by the flesh?" Galatians 3:3 NKJV

"Thus says the LORD: "Cursed *is* the man who trusts in man And makes flesh his strength, Whose heart departs from the LORD. For he shall be like a shrub in the desert, And shall not see when good comes, But shall inhabit the parched places in the wilderness, *In* a salt land *which is* not inhabited. "Blessed *is* the man who trusts in the LORD, And whose hope is the LORD. For he shall be like a tree planted by the waters, Which spreads out its roots by the river, And will not fear when heat comes; But its leaf will be green, And will not be anxious in the year of drought, Nor will cease from yielding fruit." Jeremiah 17:5-8 NKJV

""I am the vine, you *are* the branches. He who abides in Me, and I in him, bears much fruit; for without Me you can do nothing." John 15:5 NKJV

...

#75

But That Looks SO TEMPTING!

I knew what God wanted me to do. I had prayed and prayed and sought Him and heard Him and sought Him more to be sure and felt really clear about His will for me with something super big in my life and ministry. But one day I saw a flyer advertising something that seemed like it could be a really good alternative to God's will.

Seemed my life could be so much easier, comfortable, more manageable, and that there would be way fewer risks and challenges if I lay God's will aside and fell for the temptation being advertised.

The Holy Spirit almost immediately brought strong conviction. I knew what to do. My life is not mine anymore. It belongs to the Lord Jesus Christ. I no longer live for self. I live for God. I LIVE FOR JESUS!

I would continue down God's pathway of righteousness – of His ways and of His will for me. And I would rely on God and His Holy Spirit and His Word, the Bible, to keep me on the right path. His. The narrow one, yes. The right one. His. For His name's sake. Amen!

Friend, please don't walk down the broad pathway of this world. Please turn from your sins, believe in Jesus Christ as Lord and in His death and resurrection, turn to God and His ways, receive the promise of forever life with God, and walk down His pathway of righteousness as you love and serve the Lord with every ounce of your heart, Amen, Hallelujah, AMEN!

When temptation comes, turn away from it in the strength of Christ for the glory of Christ and continue down the Lord's pathway. Even as so much of this world lives with its back turned to God walking down the pathway of wickedness and rebellion against God, you may feel oh, but there are so few it seems who walk down God's narrow pathway. But remember, friend, you will not walk His pathway alone. Walk in the presence of God almighty, AMEN!

"Or do you not know that your body is the temple of the Holy Spirit who is in you, whom you have from God, and you are not your own? For you were bought at a price; therefore glorify God in your body and in your spirit, which are God's." 1 Corinthians 6:19-20 NKJV

"and He died for all, that those who live should live no longer for themselves, but for Him who died for them and rose again." 2 Corinthians 5:15 NKJV

""Enter by the narrow gate; for wide is the gate and broad is the way that leads to destruction, and there are many who go in by it. Because narrow is the gate and difficult is the way which leads to life, and there are few who find it." Matthew 7:13-14 NKJV

"The LORD is my shepherd; I shall not want. He makes me to lie down in green pastures; He leads me beside the still waters. He restores my soul; He leads me in the paths of righteousness For His name's sake." Psalms 23:1-3 NKJV

"Your word is a lamp to my feet And a light to my path." Psalms 119:105 NKJV

...

#76

Where Is God Calling You?

"Are you going to hide here, or are you going to go where I am sending you?" the Holy Spirit spoke to my heart.

I faced a big decision. Stay in an easy, secure, comfortable, familiar, beautiful, and virtually risk-free ministry location. Or pray big, pack up my belongings and beloved special needs ministry dogs, and head off for my next major ministry location on the road for Jesus with a stop along the way. Hmm, what to do?

My flesh would have held onto the former in a heartbeat. But I no longer live to please my flesh. I live to love and glorify God. I LIVE FOR JESUS now. The way I should have all along. The way we all should. So as extremely hard as it would be on my flesh, I knew what I needed to do. Humble myself, deny my flesh's craving for comfort, ease, familiarity, and what appeared to be super low-risk, take up my little cross, and follow Jesus (Luke 9:23).

This message isn't merely about when God calls us to something really big in a new geographical location. It's about the lifestyle of following Jesus.

See, believing in God is not merely an intellectual exercise in which we simply repent and put our faith in Jesus as Lord. It's a way of life. If we really believe He is Lord and in His death and resurrection, whereby we receive God's forgiveness of our sins and the promise of everlasting life with Him, we are to bear fruit of a life lived for Him. Our faith is to show forth works. Our lives are to show forth that we no longer live for self but that we LIVE FOR JESUS (2 Cor. 5:15).

Every day, we face choices and decisions regarding whether to follow our flesh, the world, and the devil – or whether to humbly, lovingly, and faithfully follow the Lord and His will for us.

Whether God calls us to Africa to serve there, to walk across the room and pray for a spouse who has just been mean to us, to share the Gospel message with three friends at school, to pray and fast for the world for the next three days, to call a bunch of people who could use love and encouragement, to cook for a neighbor just widowed, whatever the case may be, will we strive to please our flesh and do what makes us happy, content, at ease, and comfortable, or will we forsake all for the Lord and follow Him?

If you are clear about what God is calling you to do whether it be something this very day, or something really big down the road, whether small or humongous, please say YES and with love, joy, and thanksgiving follow the Holy Spirit as He leads you forth!

""…but declared first to those in Damascus and in Jerusalem, and throughout all the region of Judea, and *then* to the Gentiles, that they should repent, turn to God, and do works befitting repentance." Acts 26:19-20 NKJV

"Therefore bear fruits worthy of repentance…And even now the ax is laid to the root of the trees. Therefore every tree which does not bear good fruit is cut down and thrown into the fire."" Luke 3:8-9 NKJV

"You believe that there is one God. You do well. Even the demons believe—and tremble! But do you want to know, O foolish man, that faith without works is dead? Was not Abraham our father justified by works when he offered Isaac his son on the altar? Do you see that faith was working together with his works, and by works faith was made perfect? And the Scripture was fulfilled which says, "ABRAHAM BELIEVED GOD, AND IT WAS ACCOUNTED TO HIM FOR RIGHTEOUSNESS." And he was called the friend of God. You see then that a man is justified by works, and not by faith only." James 2:19-24 NKJV

…

#77

He Stole My Joy!

"Don't let him steal your joy," I heard the Holy Spirit speak to my heart.

Joy, one of God's beautiful blessings, is a fruit of His Spirit who lives in His followers. The joy of the Lord is not conditional on the world around us and on our life's circumstances. Jesus' followers have access to joy 24-7 through the Lord.

But just as the Lord was warning me not to do, we can allow our joy to be stolen. The devil in his mission to steal, kill, and destroy (John 10:10) uses temptations, attacks, deception, lies, etc. to try to wreck our relationship with the Lord, to get our focus off Jesus, to get us off track, to get us out of God's will, to get us into sin, to get us focused on self not Jesus, to get us bogged down in worry, anxiety, fear, anger, hatred, vengeance, bitterness, hurt, etc., and to essentially steal from us the love, hope, peace, light, grace, mercy, forgiveness, strength, wisdom we are promised in the Lord.

What should we do? Love the Lord with all our hearts, live in obedience to Him, keep our thoughts, mouths, and actions pure for Him, resist the devil, guard our hearts, take all thoughts captive, keep our focus on the Lord and the Bible and return our focus to Him when we have lost our focus, repent when we need to repent, and, above all else, learn to abide in Him.

Abide? Believe in Him, trust in Him, rest in Him, look to Him, pray to Him, seek Him, fellowship with Him, read the Bible and live by it, put our hope in Him, put our confidence in Him, put our expectation in Him, meditate on Him and on the Bible, praise Him, honor Him, rejoice in Him, worship Him, serve Him, glorify Him, commune with Him, cry out to Him, listen to Him, spend time with Him, find peace in Him, find comfort in Him, follow Him, and experience and enjoy JOY in Him. Hallelujah!

Far too often I have allowed the devil to steal my joy. I'm tired of giving up this beautiful blessing that belongs to me in Christ. I resolve to do a much better job of abiding in Him and enjoying the joy of Jesus, AMEN!

How about you?

"But the fruit of the Spirit is love, joy, peace, longsuffering, kindness, goodness, faithfulness, gentleness, self-control. Against such there is no law." Galatians 5:22-23 NKJV

"For the weapons of our warfare *are* not carnal but mighty in God for pulling down strongholds, casting down arguments and every high thing that exalts itself against the knowledge of God, bringing every thought into captivity to the obedience of Christ, and being ready to punish all disobedience when your obedience is fulfilled." 2 Corinthians 10:4-6 NKJV

"Therefore submit to God. Resist the devil and he will flee from you. Draw near to God and He will draw near to you. Cleanse *your* hands, *you* sinners; and purify *your* hearts, *you* double-minded. Lament and mourn and weep! Let your laughter be turned to mourning and *your* joy to gloom. Humble yourselves in the sight of the Lord, and He will lift you up." James 4:7-10 NKJV

"Keep your heart with all diligence, For out of it *spring* the issues of life." Proverbs 4:23 NKJV

. . .

#78

Don't Get Caught Up in Drama!

I know all about being a drama queen. I was one for decades. Drama this. Drama that. I got caught up in lots of other people's drama, and I continually created tons of my own and dragged anyone I could into it. Drama is dangerous, and here is why.

The devil comes to steal, kill, and destroy (John 10:10), and he uses drama to tempt us, distract us, get us off course, get our focus off the Lord, lure us into being self-absorbed, live for self instead of LIVE FOR JESUS, fail to love the Lord with all our hearts and to love others, disobey God, be prideful, get us to distract others from God, and on and on. But we can't blame the devil. We're responsible for taking the devil's bait and getting caught up in drama – or not.

This very day as I write this, by God's grace alone, I am choosing to not get caught up in some big drama around me. This is in obedience to God in His strength not in my weakness. Because I am not getting involved in the drama, I am free to love, serve, and worship the Lord with all my heart! Goodbye drama, hello Jesus!

Want to join me? Let us strive daily to humble ourselves and stay out of the drama and stay on God's pathway of righteousness. Amen!

"You will keep *him* in perfect peace, *Whose* mind *is* stayed *on You,* Because he trusts in You." Isaiah 26:3 NKJV

"He restores my soul; He leads me in the paths of righteousness For His name's sake." Psalms 23:3 NKJV

"But let none of you suffer as a murderer, a thief, an evildoer, or as a busybody in other people's matters." 1 Peter 4:15 NKJV

#79

Jesus and Peanut Butter Dog Toys

Not even 6 am yet, and I was delighted to see the jubilant joy of my senior special needs ministry dogs as they excitedly waited for me to set their big Kong toys down on the floor for them which I had just filled with part of their daily delicious supplement and yummy gooey peanut butter. Then something powerful, tragic, and convicting dawned on me.

My beloved paralyzed dog Miss Mercy hit by likely a truck years ago and Grace dumped at a gas station and hit by two cars long ago show more love, joy, thanksgiving, and excitement over their special morning treats which last for about 10 minutes than I and lots of other believers in the Lord Jesus Christ show ongoing love, joy, thanksgiving, and excitement to and about the Lord, our forever relationship with Him, and His endless blessings.

How delighted I was to see the love, joy, thanksgiving, and excitement of my sweet dogs in response to my giving them something so short-lived to enjoy. I can't imagine how much delight we must bring the Lord when we continually show Him love, joy, thanksgiving, and excitement over His giving us now and forever with Him – and how much we must break His heart when we do not.

Today and every day let us strive to bless the Lord with love, joy, thanksgiving, excitement, praise, honor, obedience, service, pleasure, and glory of which He is worthy now and forevermore, AMEN! Hallelujah! Amen, amen, amen!

"Rejoice in the Lord always. Again I will say, rejoice!" Philippians 4:4 NKJV

#80

NOW Is the Time to Forgive

Forgiveness is not something to be postponed. It's not something to do when we feel like it. When we want to forgive. When we feel better about someone. When time has passed and we don't hurt so much. When we think differently about the person who betrayed us. Forgiveness isn't to come when we've had time to work through all our emotions about what happened. Forgiveness doesn't have an appointed time in the future. NOW is the time to forgive. Here is why.

God's greatest commands are to love Him with all our hearts and to love one another. And God commands us to forgive. Not only that, but He makes clear He will not forgive us if we do not forgive others. Forgiveness is not to be contingent on this, that, or the other i.e. our circumstances, thoughts, and feelings. Forgiveness is to be contingent on the Lord Jesus Christ.

And lest you think it's impossible to forgive someone, rest assured God gives us all we need – strength and the ability to forgive included – to live a godly life.

Please, friend, obey God almighty. Turn from your sins. Believe in Jesus Christ as Lord and that He died for your sins and was raised from the dead. Turn to God and His ways. Henceforth LIVE FOR JESUS and no longer for self. Live according to God's ways not the world's ways. Love the Lord with every ounce of your heart. Be totally devoted to the Lord now and forever. Love others as yourself. And don't wait another minute. Forgive. Forgive, forgive, forgive. In the strength of Jesus, with the love of Jesus, by the power of the Holy Spirit of God who lives in God's followers, for the glory of Jesus, AMEN!

"And forgive us our debts, As we forgive our debtors. And do not lead us into temptation, But deliver us from the evil one. For Yours is the kingdom and the power and the glory forever. Amen.

"For if you forgive men their trespasses, your heavenly Father will also forgive you. But if you do not forgive men their trespasses, neither will your Father forgive your trespasses." Matthew 6:12-15 NKJV

"as His divine power has given to us all things that pertain to life and godliness, through the knowledge of Him who called us by glory and virtue," 2 Peter 1:3 NKJV

"I can do all things through Christ who strengthens me." Philippians 4:13 NKJV

...

#81

Not Hating is NOT Enough

God tells us in His Word that if we profess to love Him but hate someone we are liars. But God doesn't just tell us NOT to hate people. He doesn't tell us merely to tolerate people. He commands us to LOVE others.

Well this is a pretty tall order, don't you think? Sometimes we may even believe this to be impossible. Certain people we're just bound to hate, right? Or at the very most to muster up the strength to simply like them. But in all honesty there may be certain people throughout our lives there is just no way possible we can imagine wanting to love or even having the ability to love. Oh, but friend, please consider this.

God gives us the ability by the power of His Holy Spirit who lives inside His followers and through the truth and wisdom of the Bible to obey Him.

When we humble ourselves before God almighty with the genuine desire to love, obey, praise, worship, serve, and glorify Him as we should, when we cry out to Him in prayer, when we enjoy an intimate relationship with the Lord through faith in the Lord Jesus Christ and a life devoted to Him, when we spend time in His presence and in His Word, God will enable us to obey Him in all matters including when it comes to loving those apart from God we would otherwise hate!

"We love Him because He first loved us. If someone says, "I love God," and hates his brother, he is a liar; for he who does not love his brother whom he has seen, how can he love God whom he has not seen? And this commandment we have from Him: that he who loves God *must* love his brother also." 1 John 4:19-21 NKJV

"I can do all things through Christ who strengthens me." Philippians 4:13 NKJV

"as His divine power has given to us all things that *pertain* to life and godliness, through the knowledge of Him who called us by glory and virtue," 2 Peter 1:3 NKJV

...

#82

Total Surrender to God

For years I wasn't surrendered to God in the least. Then I was a little bit surrendered to Him. Today I am totally surrendered to the Lord. I am a totally devoted follower of the Lord Jesus Christ. Now this doesn't mean I don't stumble and fall. It doesn't mean I am perfect. I am anything but. But it means my heart's cry is to love and serve the Lord with all my heart. And

I finally understand God didn't create us to live for self according to the world's ways. He created us to live totally surrendered to Him according to His ways as He teaches us in the Bible.

I am compelled to challenge you with this question.

Are you totally surrendered to God almighty? The ONLY way to heaven is through the Lord Jesus Christ who died on the cross to pay our sin punishment of death, hell, and the lake of fire in eternal torment and was raised from the dead. So all who turn from our sins, believe in Him as Lord and in His death and resurrection, genuinely turning to God and His ways, are forgiven, indwelt by His Holy Spirit, and promised a forever relationship with God.

This is not about saying a little prayer and having a one-time emotional experience and going to church on Sundays. It's about turning from a lifestyle of sin and turning to the Lord and living a lifestyle of total surrender to the Lord God almighty.

If your heart and life are not totally surrendered to God, now is the time. Turn, turn, turn to the Lord! Believe in Jesus Christ as Lord and devote your life to the Lord now and forevermore, AMEN!

""Not everyone who says to Me, 'Lord, Lord,' shall enter the kingdom of heaven, but he who does the will of My Father in heaven. Many will say to Me in that day, 'Lord, Lord, have we not prophesied in Your name, cast out demons in Your name, and done many wonders in Your name?' And then I will declare to them, 'I never knew you; depart from Me, you who practice lawlessness!'" Matthew 7:21-23 NKJV

""Enter by the narrow gate; for wide *is* the gate and broad *is* the way that leads to destruction, and there are many who go in by it. Because narrow *is* the gate and difficult *is* the way which leads to life, and there are few who find it." Matthew 7:13-14 NKJV

"and He died for all, that those who live should live no longer for themselves, but for Him who died for them and rose again." 2 Corinthians 5:15 NKJV

. . .

#83

When the Devil Tries to Turn You Back

"Be very, very careful," the Holy Spirit spoke to my heart. "The enemy is going to try to turn you back."

Less than 48 hours after arriving at my latest location on the road for Jesus and ministry for nearly 5 years, albeit just a 2-week stop on my way to my next big location, here I sit writing this. The Lord just gave me an ultra clear warning which does not surprise me in the least. I have loads of experience starting to move forward in the Lord's instructions for me in life and ministry and facing tough opposition from the devil as he has tried brutally for years to get me to go backwards to my old life instead of going forward following Jesus. The biggest battles have usually been when the Lord has made clear His will for me concerning really big steps forward like writing a new book for Him or driving a long distance to a new location where He intends for me to do a great deal of ministry work.

So what does this have to do with you? The devil in his 3-fold mission to steal, kill, and destroy (John 10:10) goes all out to keep people from believing in and following the Lord Jesus Christ, to try to wreak havoc on our relationships with the Lord once we enter into them, and to try to stop us from fulfilling God's will for our lives.

One ploy the devil seems to try with lots of us is to try to turn us back. To a lifestyle of sin, to people, places, and things God has told us to leave behind, to places of comfort and ease and familiarity so we cling to all that instead of cleave to God, to anything or anyone in the past God wants us to let go in order to move forward following Him and His will for us, etc.

When the devil tries to turn you back, I want to encourage you with this. Cry out to God almighty, spend time in His presence, pray, pray, pray, study and live by His Word, ask for and receive a fresh infilling of God's Holy Spirit, praise and worship the Lord, follow the leading of His Spirit in the strength of Christ for the glory of Christ, and seek prayer and encouragement from God's followers if/when/as the Lord so leads you.

Please don't follow the voice and temptations of the devil as he tries to turn you back. Turn to the Lord and go forth wherever and however He so leads you. For the glory of God, AMEN!

I love God's words to Joshua!

"Only be strong and very courageous, that you may observe to do according to all the law which Moses My servant commanded you; do not turn from it to the right hand or to the left, that you may prosper wherever you go. This Book of the Law shall not depart from your mouth, but you shall meditate in it day and night, that you may observe to do according to all that is written in it. For then you will make your way prosperous, and then you will have good success. Have I not commanded you? Be strong and of good courage; do not be afraid, nor be dismayed, for the LORD your God *is* with you wherever you go."" Joshua 1:7-9 NKJV

I am so encouraged hearing Jesus say this:

"If anyone serves Me, let him follow Me; and where I am, there My servant will be also. If anyone serves Me, him *My* Father will honor." John 12:26 NKJV

Please find more encouragement in these verses that follow!

"For as many as are led by the Spirit of God, these are sons of God." Romans 8:14 NKJV

"But he who enters by the door is the shepherd of the sheep. To him the doorkeeper opens, and the sheep hear his voice; and he calls his own sheep by name and leads them out. And when he brings out his own sheep, he goes before them; and the sheep follow him, for they know his voice. Yet they will by no means follow a stranger, but will flee from him, for they do not know the voice of strangers.'" John 10:2-5 NKJV

...

#84

Being Thankful in a Darkening World

It takes about 2 minutes of focusing on the world news to see the truth as God shows us in the Bible that the world due to the sinfulness of humanity is darkening, and it takes just seconds for many of us like myself to get swallowed up in negativity, anxiety, ungratefulness, complaining, self-pity, and the like.

When we focus on the evil of this world and on the hardness of our trials and tribulations, we can get swept away by the darkness and likely do nothing more than contribute to it whether in or actions or simply in our

147 - Live for Jesus

words, thoughts and attitudes or even in all of this. But we have a choice as the Lord so often reminds me.

We can focus on the darkness and think about it, talk about it, respond in our feelings to it, and react to it with our own sinfulness. Or we can turn our hearts and minds to the one true God, God almighty, light of this world, the God who is love, the God of hope, the God of comfort, the God of peace, Savior of the world, God who loves us so much He sent His only Son Jesus to the cross to die for us and to raise Him from the dead. So all who turn from our sins, believe in Jesus Christ as Lord, and in His death and resurrection, truly turning our lives over to God and His ways, are forgiven, indwelt by God's Holy Spirit, promised a forever relationship with the Lord, and are to love, revere, fear, honor, praise, worship, serve, obey, and glorify the Lord forevermore! To experience and enjoy the Lord in an intimate, splendorous, light-, hope-, joy-, peace-, and passion-filled relationship with Him right here on this earth even as the world darkens – and forevermore!

Friend, when we turn away from the darkness and turn to Jesus Christ, light of this world, we have reason to be filled with love, peace, hope, joy – and THANKSGIVING to the Lord most high!

This world will one day be gone, and there will be a new heavens and a new earth. And for those who turn to Jesus Christ as Lord, who follow Jesus Christ as Lord, who live for Jesus Christ as Lord, who live according to God's ways as He teaches us in the Bible for God's glory, who are filled with and led by God's Holy Spirit for the glory of Christ, we have an exceedingly wonderful blessed promise.

The promise right here, right now, even in this very moment, and the next moment, and all the moments for now and eternity to come, of intimate fellowship with the Lord. And we can, and should, REJOICE and BE

THANKFUL that Jesus Christ is Lord forever and that we are His forevermore! Hallelujah, AMEN!

Let us humble ourselves before God almighty, let us turn from our sins, let us become and remain totally devoted followers of the Lord Jesus Christ, let us make a conscious effort to set our hearts and minds upon God and His goodness and His infinite blessings, and let us BE THANKFUL for the Lord and to the Lord now, this very day, tomorrow, and forever and ever, AMEN!

"Then Jesus spoke to them again, saying, "I am the light of the world. He who follows Me shall not walk in darkness, but have the light of life.""
John 8:12 NKJV

I cannot encourage you enough to spend time each and every day alone in the presence of God almighty, and in the Bible, loving, praising, magnifying, singing to, seeking, praying to, hearing, obeying, communing with, trusting in, abiding in, resting in, rejoicing in, spending time with, hoping in, worshiping, glorifying, and enjoying the Lord.

But PLEASE do not limit your time with the Lord to a set-apart time. Please day in and day out enjoy an intimate relationship with Jesus Christ as Lord, ever looking to God, praying, hearing, following, learning of Him, striving to please Him, abiding, abiding, abiding in Him, oh yes! AMEN!

...

#85
Thank God for New Vision!

Praise the Lord, as I write this, I am wearing my new prescription reading glasses. I love them. I tried prescription reading glasses once before but had a bad experience with the company and ended up with glasses that caused more trouble than good. My vision has gone downhill as I have aged. I am sad to say I didn't realize how bad things had gotten until I was editing a book I had written and realized my blurry vision was making writing and editing pretty hard. Still, it was a long while until I finally surrendered and went to Walmart to get a vision test and order glasses.

I am so thankful to the Lord for providing my glasses and for the help He sent me and for the money to get them. But the good, new, and clear vision I have now when I wear my glasses is nothing compared with the "good, new, and clear vision" God has given me in life. And for this I am exceedingly thankful to the Lord!

Can you relate to any of this? God has given me the "good, new, and clear vision" to see my sin, to realize my need to repent and be forgiven, to see and know and receive His love, to see and appreciate His majesty and splendor and beauty, to see and appreciate His grace and mercy and kindness and care and compassion and goodness and wisdom. To see where I need to grow, to see how nothing I am without Him, to see when I need to purify myself. To see my continual need for Him, to see His blessedness and blessings, to see His goodness and to acknowledge and praise Him for it. To read the Bible and learn to live by it, to see others' needs and how He wants me to love and serve them, and on and on. He has most assuredly given me new vision!

When we repent and receive Jesus Christ as Lord, truly surrendering our lives to God, He makes us "new creatures". And, as new creatures, we are essentially given new vision, don't you think? The ability to see what we couldn't see before. And with this comes an amazing opportunity to tell and show the Lord how very thankful we are! For our new God-given vision, AMEN!

"Therefore, if anyone *is* in Christ, *he is* a new creation; old things have passed away; behold, all things have become new." 2 Corinthians 5:17 NKJV

...

#86

The Psychic Tragedy

I don't go to psychics. Okay, that is not entirely true. Sometimes God sends me to psychics, fortune tellers, palm readers, etc. kind of people to talk to them about Jesus and give them Gospel tracts. This time around, God sent a psychic to me. And here is the tragedy.

I crossed paths with a psychic in my life on the road for Jesus, and in the few minutes we chatted he noticed something very true about myself that I think most people wouldn't notice. He was right. Now please understand this truth. Any of the practices I have just mentioned are part of countless practices worldwide that involve sin against God and worship of false gods and false beliefs. ALL of this needs to be repented of, and we all whether psychic, fortune teller, etc. or not need to turn from our sins to Jesus Christ as Lord, believe in His death and resurrection, and turn to God and His ways. This psychic simply took the time and paid enough attention and had the sensitivity to notice this particular thing about me.

So what is the tragedy? The psychic took the time to observe me and care and be sensitive and compassionate, whereas countless believers in Jesus myself included can fall very far short in taking the time in our busy lives to show love, compassion, care, kindness, and sensitivity to others. Many of us are simply too self-absorbed and too focused on our own plans and agendas each day to see our fellow humans as those needing love, kindness, help, compassion, support, and sensitivity.

Friend, I strive daily now to walk in the love of Jesus toward all – and to repent when I need to. Please join me. Please do the same. This is so very crucial and fundamental in living for Jesus!

"Though I speak with the tongues of men and of angels, but have not love, I have become sounding brass or a clanging cymbal. And though I have *the gift of* prophecy, and understand all mysteries and all knowledge, and though I have all faith, so that I could remove mountains, but have not love, I am nothing. And though I bestow all my goods to feed *the poor,* and though I give my body to be burned, but have not love, it profits me nothing. Love suffers long *and* is kind; love does not envy; love does not parade itself, is not puffed up; does not behave rudely, does not seek its own, is not provoked, thinks no evil; does not rejoice in iniquity, but rejoices in the truth; bears all things, believes all things, hopes all things, endures all things. Love never fails. But whether *there are* prophecies, they will fail; whether *there are* tongues, they will cease; whether *there is* knowledge, it will vanish away." 1 Corinthians 13:1-8 NKJV

…

#87

Choose to Rejoice

If there is anything I have learned about rejoicing it is this. God in the Bible calls us to rejoice CONTINUALLY, the way to rejoice CONTINUALLY is to REJOICE in the Lord and in our relationship with Him and in His amazingness and endless goodness and blessings, rejoicing is a CHOICE, no matter the world's woes and our personal struggles we can REJOICE when we turn our hearts and minds to the Lord and the Bible and His countless blessings, and we SHOULD CHOOSE TO REJOICE – ALWAYS!

Rest assured I can fall into negativity, complaining, moaning, griping, groaning, discouragement, downheartedness, heavy sorrow, depressing thoughts, self-pity, and spiraling downhill mentally and emotionally in a heartbeat – and getting stuck there! I have been prone to this my whole life. It feels absolutely awful, and when I'm in it I am far away from obeying God's greatest commands to love Him with all my heart and to love others as myself. Why? Because I am consumed with self and can't see past me and my dark thoughts and burdensome emotions!

But God in His awesome love and mercy reminds me on a regular basis to get rid of the heaviness, to repent of any and all sin in my heart, words, and actions, to turn to Him and the Bible, and to REJOICE IN THE LORD JESUS CHRIST!

Given the state of the world right now, and given how many people are suffering to one degree or another, I can't think of a better time for us all to make a conscious effort each and every day to be totally devoted to the Lord Jesus Christ, to REJOICE IN THE LORD each and every day, and to strive day in and day out to bring love, praise, pleasure, honor, adoration, worship, obedience, service, thanksgiving, and glory to the Lord most high now and forevermore. HALLELUJAH, oh rejoice, rejoice, rejoice, rejoice, AMEN! Praise the Lord! To the Lord be the glory AMEN!

"Rejoice in the Lord always. Again I will say, rejoice!" Philippians 4:4 NKJV

"This *is* the day the LORD has made; We will rejoice and be glad in it."

Psalms 118:24 NKJV

I strongly encourage you as you read the Bible to take note of the enormous number of references to JOY and REJOICING!

…

A Special Note Before You Continue On…

Please note I don't write my books with an outline and plan. I write message by message as best I can discern the Lord leading me. When it is time to do what usually is only a very light edit of all the individual messages put together into a book, I am sometimes surprised by what I find. See, I don't have the really good memory I once had. It is not uncommon for me to forget what I have written write after writing it! And I am blessed with being gifted by God with writing in such a way that the messages pour out of me sometimes so much so it's hard to keep up with writing and publishing them!

This said, when I realized I had two messages in this book one after another on fear, my instinct was to consider getting rid of one of them and simply replacing it with another message. But instead, I have chosen to trust the Lord that He has a purpose for them both and with placing them one after another. So please open your heart and see how the Lord might speak through the next two messages, and with the others that follow! And may you be encouraged, inspired – and challenged. To the Lord be the glory, AMEN!

…

#88

But God I Am SCARED!

When I was a little girl, long before I believed in God, I was PETRIFIED of spending the night at friends' houses. I didn't want to spend a single night away from home. I would call my parents and get them to bring me home. I was terrified of going to sleep-away camp but finally did. I confess I have struggled with loads of fear, worry, and anxiety my whole life. Isn't it something I write this as I am days away from packing up my special needs ministry dogs, most of my life's belongings, my ministry equipment, and the dogs' wheelchair and supplies all into one vehicle and heading off to another season of streets ministry in New York City as well as neighboring northern New Jersey? And isn't it something April 2022 will mark five years on the road full-time for the Lord and ministry? Utterly miraculous, only and all by the grace of God, and with this testimony comes a powerful message for us all.

The world judges us for being afraid and teaches us to hide our fears and pridefully put on an appearance of strength, confidence, and courage. But God has taught me to handle fear, worry, and anxiety in an entirely different manner.

The Lord has taught me to humble myself, to come to Him with my fear, worry, and anxiety, to pour out my heart to Him about this and everything else in my heart, to confess my weakness to Him, to spend time in His presence praising, worshiping, adoring, singing to, seeking, praying to, waiting on, hearing, and receiving wisdom, courage, strength, comfort, healing, and all else I need from Him.

I was broken beyond human hope and repair for decades, didn't believe God even existed, had no sense of significance nor purpose on this earth, contemplated killing myself on and off for about 20 years, have struggled with an endless stream of things to this very day, and can't think of a more least likely candidate to be on the road full-time for Jesus telling the world about Him. I literally can't draw one breath let alone fulfill one ounce of my life's calling for God without Him.

The greatest lesson I have learned about fear is to admit I have it and to go to God with it, to cast it upon Him, to receive all I need from Him, to not allow fear to stop me from doing what God calls me to do day by day, to not let fear reign in my heart and life, to yield to the Holy Spirit of God as He empowers and leads and guides and provides for me, and to press on in life and ministry in the strength of Christ for the glory of Christ, Hallelujah!

I praise God for each and every person who prays for me and Good News Ministry, but I do not give glory to humans for lovingly praying for me that I might continue following Jesus day by day. I give glory to God almighty who loves me despite my struggles with fear and all else and lovingly, mercifully patiently teaches and enables me to faithfully follow Him each and every day and forevermore, AMEN!

Please, friend, if you struggle with fear as I do, don't let fear stop you from living the life God is calling you to live. Turn from your sins, believe Jesus Christ is Lord and in His death and resurrection, turn to God and His ways, be forgiven, be promised a forever relationship with God instead of hell and the lake of fire forever, ask for and receive the gift of God's Holy Spirit, spend time alone with God and read the Bible each and every day, be a totally devoted follower of the Lord Jesus Christ, and let the one who reigns in your heart and life not be fear or any other sin but God almighty, glory be to the Lord, hallelujah, AMEN!

"For God has not given us a spirit of fear, but of power and of love and of a sound mind." 2 Timothy 1:7 NKJV

"And lest I should be exalted above measure by the abundance of the revelations, a thorn in the flesh was given to me, a messenger of Satan to buffet me, lest I be exalted above measure. Concerning this thing I pleaded with the Lord three times that it might depart from me. And He said to me, "My grace is sufficient for you, for My strength is made perfect in weakness." Therefore most gladly I will rather boast in my infirmities, that the power of Christ may rest upon me. Therefore I take pleasure in infirmities, in reproaches, in needs, in persecutions, in distresses, for Christ's sake. For when I am weak, then I am strong." 2 Corinthians 12:7-10 NKJV

"You will keep *him* in perfect peace, *Whose* mind *is* stayed *on You,* Because he trusts in You. Trust in the LORD forever, For in YAH, the LORD, *is* everlasting strength." Isaiah 26:3-4 NKJV

...

#89

If You Struggle with FEAR…

If you struggle with fear, please friend, don't let the devil use it to stop you from living the life God is calling you to live!

This month marks 5 years since I put my little house not far from the ocean on the market, gave most everything away, and have been on the road full-time without a permanent residence with my special needs ministry dogs ever since for the Lord and ministry. I have struggled with fear, worry, doubt, and anxiety along with lots of other huge challenges my whole life – to this very day in fact. But I have learned an incredible lesson about fear I share with you now.

We can bow down and worship fear like a god and allow it to rule and reign in our hearts and lives and let the devil use it to stop us from fulfilling God's will for our lives. Or we can humble ourselves and bow down before God almighty and no matter how hard fear and anxiety come at us choose to put our trust in God moment by moment and find our hope, strength, confidence, security, wisdom, direction, and all that we need physically, emotionally, and spiritually IN THE LORD.

When fear and anxiety threaten to take us down and out and get us to run for dear life away from God's will for our lives, we can choose instead to run to the Lord, pour out our hearts to Him – fear included – and take refuge in Him. We can find shelter in Him. We can cry out to Him, pray to Him, seek Him, read the Bible, spend time in His presence, praise and worship Him, sing to Him, adore Him, receive His love, comfort, healing, and hope, and love, love, love Him with total devotion, ever striving to bring Him praise, honor, joy, pleasure, and glory.

In my years on the road, I have ministered on death row, talked to a murderer on the street about Jesus, stayed at three hotels in a row where dead bodies were found and not fled, been yelled at, cursed at, threatened, been treated terribly, been verbally abused, ministered to criminals, been in a courtyard alone with a violent man who was about to be arrested, had no permanent home to run back to, ministered on the streets of New York City, gone up to drug addicts getting high and given them Gospel tracts, held a man in my arms who broke into the building where I was staying temporarily and now a month or so later was appeared to be overdosing, walked through an area filled with addicts on a drug that made them look like dead men and women walking, and on and on. I have left comfortable places for scary places. I have gone to new locations on the road when I was petrified. I have stayed at hotels to minister there even when my flesh was terrified.

Think I wasn't scared? Think I don't struggle with anxiety daily over a zillion different things? Oh, I most assuredly struggle with fear every day of my life. But I have learned to run to the Lord and to not bow my knee to fear. I have learned to live and breathe to love and glorify God now and forever. I am learning day by day to be a totally devoted follower of the Lord Jesus Christ. And God in Christ gives me all I need to live for Him including the ability to keep following Him in life and ministry no matter how hard the devil comes at me with fear.

Friend, please, I implore you, don't let fear stop you from being a totally devoted follower of Jesus. Live and breathe for God. Pour out your heart to Him. Follow Him humbly and faithfully. Let Him reign in your life. Submit to God. Don't surrender to the fear. Live surrendered to God. Now and forevermore, LIVE FOR JESUS, hallelujah, glory be to God, AMEN!

"I can do all things through Christ who strengthens me." Philippians 4:13 NKJV

"Jesus said to him, "If you can believe, all things *are* possible to him who believes."" Mark 9:23 NKJV

"Therefore submit to God. Resist the devil and he will flee from you. Draw near to God and He will draw near to you…" James 4:7-8 NKJV

…

#90

Amazing Police Testimony!

Within about 24 hours of arriving in my latest location of being on the road for Jesus full-time for about 5 years with my special needs ministry dogs, I did my usual when I arrive at a new location even if it is one I have been sent by God before as this one was. I had left behind coastal South Carolina in sunny 70 degree weather at the beach with my beloved dogs to spend two weeks in grey, windy, and cold Virginia after spending 11 hours in the car. Two weeks later, I spent another 5 hours in the car to arrive in what in the days to come would turn out to be freezing cold, grey, rainy, and windy weather. And I am so sensitive to cold that I can wake in the night in a heated room at 78 degrees and feel really cold.

My usual at a new location? I usually get really scared, feel really overwhelmed, think about running back to wherever I came from, question whether I have lost my mind, wondered if I was wrong about where I felt God had sent me, and want to escape as quickly as possible and start imagining where I can RUN.

How could I possibly have the strength as a middle-aged woman on the road for all these years wiped out time and again by this crazy world combined with my personal challenges and the stress of my ministry work? Oh, but what a beautiful blessing God brought me this time around!

When I looked out my open hotel room door and saw two police officers in bullet-proof vests, I didn't panic. I am used to police coming and going at the budget hotels where I stay and often do much ministry. Words came bursting from my mouth which is typical of me.

"Want to come meet my dogs?" I essentially said as I walked over to them.

I am sure the police officers were taken back. Nevertheless they walked over with me to my room to meet my beloved dogs. As most people are, they were enamored by my paralyzed wheelchair doggy Miss Mercy. And shy Gracie in her usual fashion stood back at a distance to see if she could trust them enough to come up for a hello.

We chatted a bit about the dogs. Somehow, in the midst of it, I did something a bit odd especially given the officers were in uniform and bullet proof vests. I looked down at the wrist of one of the officers. That's when I saw it. I should wear glasses but usually only do when driving. So I asked to make sure I saw correctly. Sure enough. Amazing what God had sent me courtesy of a bullet proof-vested police officer.

On his wrist? A wristband with a reference to a Bible verse. Philippians 4:13.

"I can do all things through Christ who strengthens me." Philippians 4:13 NKJV

I was in awe once again of the Lord's wondrousness and blessedness and His amazing love and care.

I told the officers how moved I was by receiving that verse, and the officer with the wristband commented how it seemed God had essentially sent him to the hotel that day to bring me that verse. Oh, most assuredly!

I could be wrong, but it would not surprise me in the least if someone God leads to read this message needs this exact verse. Reminding us all that through the Lord Jesus Christ, when our lives are surrendered to Him, we can receive all we need – strength included – to do all to which the Lord calls us. Oh, praise the Lord for this blessed little testimony! May you be greatly, greatly encouraged – AMEN!

…

#91

Say Yes to God!

I was brushing my teeth or my hair, I can't remember which, i.e. doing something totally trivial, when something flashed in my heart. A thought, that was all. Right? Wrong. I realized almost immediately the Holy Spirit had placed something in my heart. God's will for me with something. And my response was immediate. No! Resistance! Rebellion! It didn't last long. Maybe 10 seconds or so. Because now, at long last, I know better than this. I spent years calling myself a believer in the Lord Jesus Christ and living for self rather than for Jesus. Things are different now. Now I LIVE FOR JESUS!

I understand God's truth. His followers are to follow Him. Loving and serving Him with all our hearts. Being totally devoted to Him. Living in obedience to Him and repenting along the way when we need to. Humbling ourselves before Him. Purifying ourselves continually. Living and breathing to love, worship, praise, adore, seek, pray to, hear through the Bible and by His Holy Spirit speaking to our hearts in line with the Bible, obey, experience, enjoy, abide in, serve, and glorify the Lord. So when it comes to the Lord making clear His will to us regarding absolutely anything, there is only one right way to respond.

Say YES to God! And no to the devil. No to the flesh. No to anyone who is trying to convince us to go against the will of God almighty. We are to say YES to the Lord. Without hesitation. With no debate, resistance, or rebellion. We are to submit ourselves utterly – and lovingly and reverently – TO THE LORD!

If you are clear God is telling you to do something, if you have prayed and heard Him, if you made sure what you have heard lines up with the Bible as it should, if you have sought godly counsel from others if and as the Lord has led you, if you know that you know that you know God has called you to do something, please do the right thing.

Say YES to God – and walk forth in loving, humble, blessed obedience to the Lord God almighty, Hallelujah, AMEN!

Obedience to God is more important than imaginable. We are to obey the Lord as far as His commands to us in the Bible are concerned. And we are to obey Him as His Holy Spirit who lives in His followers leads us personally in our individual lives. The following verses are a wonderful and strong reminder to live in obedience to our Father in heaven, AMEN!

""But why do you call Me 'Lord, Lord,' and not do the things which I say? Whoever comes to Me, and hears My sayings and does them, I will show you whom he is like: He is like a man building a house, who dug deep and laid the foundation on the rock. And when the flood arose, the stream beat vehemently against that house, and could not shake it, for it was founded on the rock. But he who heard and did nothing is like a man who built a house on the earth without a foundation, against which the stream beat vehemently; and immediately it fell. And the ruin of that house was great."" Luke 6:46-49 NKJV

"I delight to do Your will, O my God, And Your law *is* within my heart."" Psalms 40:8 NKJV

...

#92

God's Stepping Stones

I think of stepping stones as little stones people step upon as part of the pathway to get to their ultimate destination. We may think they're not important, but they're actually very important because they are necessary for us to get from our starting place to the place we intend to go.

Stepping stones aid along the way. Each stepping stone has a significance and a place and purpose in the journey and should not be thought of us as meaningless. We should be thankful for all the stepping stones along the route to get to our destination. This is not true merely when it comes to physically walking down a pathway. This is also the case when it comes to walking with God down the pathway of righteousness He sets before us.

Sometimes God sets before us people, places, and/or things He may not intend for us to have for the rest of our lives or even long-term but instead to have for just seasons in our lives as we follow Him day by day on our life's journey with Him.

I want to encourage you to consider two things in regard to your stepping stones.

First, we should not try to hold on to people, places, and things when God makes clear it is time to move on down the pathway of life. When we are clear God has let us know that a season is over, we should humble ourselves and obey Him. We should be thankful for the time He gave us in those places and with those people doing what He gave us to do there, but we shouldn't hold on. We should let go and move on.

Second, we should not minimize the importance and significance and purpose God has for us concerning the people, places, and things He places in different seasons of our lives even if those seasons seem so very short. Just because they may have been stepping stones on our way to wherever God is leading us, we should still value each and every stepping stone along the way and be thankful to the Lord for them.

Let us value and be thankful for all and everyone God places in our lives and for all He leads us through and for each and every stepping stone along the way through the seasons of our lives as His Holy Spirit leads us down the pathway of life! Amen!

"To everything *there is* a season, A time for every purpose under heaven:" Ecclesiastes 3:1 NKJV

"And we know that all things work together for good to those who love God, to those who are the called according to *His* purpose." Romans 8:28 NKJV

"He restores my soul; He leads me in the paths of righteousness For His name's sake." Psalms 23:3 NKJV

...

#93

Are You "Moved with Compassion"?

I love how Jesus in His time on earth was described not merely as being compassionate but as being "moved with compassion." He didn't merely feel love, mercy, kindness, care, concern, and sorrow etc. for people in need. He was "moved with compassion" whereby He ACTED on His compassion to help others.

In obeying God's greatest commands to love Him with all our hearts and to love one another, we, too, should be "moved with compassion".

It is one thing for our hearts to be filled with love, mercy, kindness, care, concern, and sorrow etc. for those in need as well our hearts should be. But along with this, we should be "moved with compassion" whereby we seek and fulfill the Lord's will in loving, helping, giving to, sharing with, supporting, praying for, encouraging, etc. a world in need.

A compassionate heart is evidenced by such things as crying tears over people's suffering, pitying people who are hurting, grieving when others grieve, being heartbroken when people go through unimaginable tragedies, feeling deeply sad over people devastated by natural disasters, hurting when people hurt, truly and deeply caring about people and their needs, etc.

But let us not merely have compassionate hearts for people all around this world who hurt, suffer, hunger, are broken, are sick, dying, disabled, who are grieving, lonely, facing unbelievable trials and tribulations, etc. Let us be "moved with compassion"! Let us be moved to ACTION.

Let us pray to the Lord, let us wait on the Lord, let us hear the Lord by His Holy Spirit who lives inside His followers speaking to our hearts, and let us ACT with love and compassion as He so leads us.

Are you "moved with compassion"? Oh, may it be so! And may we not take the credit and glory for our acts of compassion. May we take the opportunities God gives us to love and serve others with compassion to GIVE GOD THE GLORY! Hallelujah! Praise the Lord! Amen!

"But when He saw the multitudes, He was moved with compassion for them, because they were weary and scattered, like sheep having no shepherd." Matthew 9:36 NKJV

"And when Jesus went out He saw a great multitude; and He was moved with compassion for them, and healed their sick." Matthew 14:14 NKJV

"Then Jesus, moved with compassion, stretched out *His* hand and touched him, and said to him, "I am willing; be cleansed."" Mark 1:41 NKJV

"And Jesus, when He came out, saw a great multitude and was moved with compassion for them, because they were like sheep not having a shepherd. So He began to teach them many things." Mark 6:34 NKJV

Please be greatly encouraged reading these incredibly beautiful and powerful words from the mouth of the Lord Jesus Christ concerning acting with love and compassion toward those in need!

"Then the King will say to those on His right hand, 'Come, you blessed of My Father, inherit the kingdom prepared for you from the foundation of the world: for I was hungry and you gave Me food; I was thirsty and you gave Me drink; I was a stranger and you took Me in; I *was* naked and you clothed Me; I was sick and you visited Me; I was in prison and you came to Me.' "Then the righteous will answer Him, saying, 'Lord, when did we see You hungry and feed *You,* or thirsty and give *You* drink? When did we see You a stranger and take *You* in, or naked and clothe *You?* Or when did we see You sick, or in prison, and come to You?' And the King will answer and say to them, 'Assuredly, I say to you, inasmuch as you did *it* to one of the least of these My brethren, you did *it* to Me.'" Matthew 25:34-40 NKJV

. . .

#94

Don't Stop Until God Says So

I was walking along the Hudson River on the Hoboken, New Jersey, side with an amazing view of the New York City skyline a little over a week after arriving in the New York City / New Jersey area as my latest stop on the road full-time for Jesus and ministry when I felt strongly compelled to stop and do a little Video Devotional called "Don't Stop Until God Says So." Only trouble was it was so windy that the poor sound quality of the video made me think I would be best to delete the Video Devotional rather than share it. But the message stayed on my heart, and I cannot help but share it with you now.

Despite my exceeding passion for loving and serving the Lord with all my heart and giving my ministry work 100%, I am strongly prone to discouragement, downheartedness, frustration, impatience, restlessness, discomfort, feeling yucky, and thinking of quitting. Even in recent days, even on this very day I write this, I have felt beaten down by cold weather, lots of grey days, wind, rain, being tremendously on my own, adjusting to my latest location, leaving behind warm weather and beach ministry in South Carolina, etc.

I have been tempted to "stop" a zillion times over the years, and I know I am not alone in wanting to stop what God has led me to start. Sometimes our flesh just doesn't want to persevere in whatever we have begun in obedience to God concerning His will for our lives. So I think this message is tremendously important.

Friend, if you are considering stopping whatever you have started for God, if you are clear about His will and have begun walking down the pathway God has set before you concerning something to which He has called you, please don't stop until – and unless – God calls you to stop.

Two verses come to mind. First, God makes clear following Him means we are not to live for ourselves any longer but for Him! Yes, we are to LIVE FOR JESUS!

"and He died for all, that those who live should live no longer for themselves, but for Him who died for them and rose again." 2 Corinthians 5:15 NKJV

Second, the Lord makes clear His followers are NOT to disobey Him. We are to OBEY HIM! The common theme in these verses? OBEDIENCE!

""But why do you call Me 'Lord, Lord,' and not do the things which I say?" Luke 6:46 NKJV

But how are we supposed to continue when we're totally worn out, feeling discouraged and down, feeling like we won't make it, are tempted to do something easier and more comfortable, can't muster up the strength, etc.?

Turn to the Lord, turn to His Word, cry out to God, dive deep into the Bible, call upon His name, pray, pray, pray, spend time alone in His presence, ask others to pray for us if and as the Lord so leads us, ask God for and receive from Him all we need to press on, and make the decision to love and obey the Lord. In the strength of Christ, for the glory of Christ, AMEN!

Please don't stop unless – and until – God says so. Rest assured He will enable you to endure and carry on if it is His will for you to do so!

"I can do all things through Christ who strengthens me." Philippians 4:13 NKJV

...

#95

When Only God Can See

A loved one essentially told me long ago we only see the little picture; God sees the whole picture. How true this is.

I can't tell you how many times in my life and ministry God has called me to do something that makes absolutely no sense, seems impossible, looks ridiculous, etc. because with my human eyes I simply can't see God's will, His plan, His purpose, how things are going to unfold, how things are going to turn out, how I am going to make it, etc. But God has so clearly spoken to my heart, and I have been so convinced of His will, and I so understand Jesus is Lord and that I am to obey Him, that I have humbled myself and made the decision to obey Him even when only God can see. In His strength, mind you. Most assuredly not in my weakness.

Examples? Selling my little house not far from the ocean, giving away most of my belongings, and hitting the road full-time for Jesus and ministry with what then were 6 ministry senior and special needs rescued dogs. Going to locations in my approximately 5 years now on the road for Jesus that made absolutely no sense to go to particularly given the distance and sacrifice involved. Writing and publishing countless messages and numerous books God put on my heart to write that seemed like a waste of time to write given in the world's eyes I am an unknown writer who does virtually no marketing, advertising, and publicity. Reaching out to people by phone God put on my heart when I had no understanding and sometimes no desire to reach out. Making decisions that went totally contrary to what I felt I should do. Oh, the list goes on.

And I can't tell you how many times God has made abundantly clear ultimately that He had a significant and important purpose and outcome in His will for me if only I would humble myself and obey. God could see the whole picture in all of this and in all of my life and in all of our lives and in all this world despite how very little we ourselves can see. Oh, how we must humble ourselves and obey Him as we learn to choose to put our trust in Him moment by moment, step by step, breath by breath.

Oh, how much I would miss in life if I lived according to what I can see, to what I understand, to what I feel and think, to others' opinions, and to the devil's temptations. But God is teaching me to live by faith in Him. And that even when I cannot see, it's okay. He can see for me as I believe I may have heard or read a Jesus follower essentially preach. My job is to simply humble myself and submit to Him.

How about you, friend? Are you living according to what you see and understand and what your flesh desires? Or, are you learning as I am to live by faith? To pray and hear God and follow Him even when you can't see where He is leading you? Please join me in learning to live by faith. To walk by faith. The way we are called to live. Trusting in Him. Obedient to Him. Believing He will lead and guide and provide for us all along the way when we put our faith in Him. Amen!

"For we walk by faith, not by sight." 2 Corinthians 5:7 NKJV

I love how Abraham is described. Talk about faith!

"By faith Abraham obeyed when he was called to go out to the place which he would receive as an inheritance. And he went out, not knowing where he was going. By faith he dwelt in the land of promise as *in* a foreign country, dwelling in tents with Isaac and Jacob, the heirs with him of the same promise; for he waited for the city which has foundations, whose builder and maker *is* God." Hebrews 11:8-10 NKJV

And here are some very well-known verses to encourage you.

"Trust in the LORD with all your heart, And lean not on your own understanding; In all your ways acknowledge Him, And He shall direct your paths." Proverbs 3:5-6 NKJV

My greatest encouragement to you is this. Find encouragement in the Lord and in the Bible and in developing a deeply intimate, deeply beautiful, ever-deepening forever relationship with the Lord!

"But without faith *it is* impossible to please *Him,* for he who comes to God must believe that He is, and *that* He is a rewarder of those who diligently seek Him." Hebrews 11:6 NKJV

…

#96

A Wild Surprise About Worship

Know what I wrote the Lord one day? I told Him this: "So wild that worship feels so good and freeing and wonderful dear Father singing to you praising you adoring you with others and very much on my own it feels amazing how is it that we're supposed to be blessing you and we get blessed in the process? Oh thank you God for the blessing and blessedness of praising and worshiping you!" Okay, please disregard the terrible grammar in my words to the Lord. I didn't intend to share them but couldn't help myself as I so wanted to share this beautiful blessing with you.

I have an amazingly beautiful, deeply intimate and passionate personal relationship with the Lord Jesus Christ. I am not simply totally devoted to the Lord outwardly in my actions as I strive to fulfill His will for my life. I am madly, passionately, indescribably in love with the Lord. And I absolutely love to tell Him how much I love Him, to spend time with Him, thank Him, adore Him, sing to Him, praise Him, serve Him, tell others about Him, and worship Him – "in spirit and in truth". In the very core of my being. In the very deepest part of me, I love to worship the Lord. Worship to me is so exceedingly more than simply singing songs of praise to God. As a loved one told me long ago, worship should be a lifestyle. Our very way of life. This I truly believe.

What I never expected in all this, however, is that the more I worship the Lord, the more I pour out my heart to the Lord in love, praise, adoration, service, and thanksgiving, the more joyful, free, and filled with hope and passion I become. In the very process of striving to bless the Lord, I get blessed. Wow! Isn't that something? Amazing, isn't it? Oh, yes!

I want to encourage you with all my heart NOT to praise, worship, and bless the Lord in a self-seeking way whereby you are doing it to feel good and be blessed by God. I want to encourage you to love and worship the Lord with all your heart because He is worthy of all our praise, love, adoration, thanksgiving, and worship 24-7 forever. And, in so doing, I believe you, too, will be blessed beyond imagination.

Oh, bless, bless, bless, praise, love, adore, thank, worship and glorify the Lord today, tomorrow, and forevermore, AMEN!

"I will bless the LORD at all times; His praise *shall* continually *be* in my mouth." Psalms 34:1 NKJV

"Bless the LORD, O my soul; And all that is within me, *bless* His holy name!" Psalms 103:1 NKJV

"But we will bless the LORD From this time forth and forevermore. Praise the LORD!" Psalms 115:18 NKJV

"But the hour is coming, and now is, when the true worshipers will worship the Father in spirit and truth; for the Father is seeking such to worship Him. God *is* Spirit, and those who worship Him must worship in spirit and truth."" John 4:23-24 NKJV

...

#97

Amazing New York City Testimony

How utterly amazing the Lord is! One day He sent me from my hotel in New Jersey as one of my locations on the road for Him and ministry full-time back into New York City for more streets ministry there. I had a phenomenal time walking for miles preaching, passing out tracts, ministering to people, praying, and worshiping the Lord as I walked. Exhausted and very ready to catch my bus back to my hotel to care for my special needs ministry dogs and excited to enjoy a plain rotisserie chicken I had just purchased from Whole Foods in my ever effort to get enough protein and put weight on to please the Lord. God changed my plans.

Right before my bus came, I noticed a homeless woman in the bus station who turns out was in the process of what appeared to be possibly overdosing from what I found out later was the drug crack. No bus station staff to help. No police around. None of the people at the bus station waiting for buses noticed and/or did anything. God gave me the amazing opportunity of staying with her for quite a long time praying for her, talking to her about Jesus, dialing 911, and working closely with the dispatcher to monitor her and relay back to him her condition. She appeared on the verge of losing consciousness and what I thought could be possible death. This was not a first for me. I have done this several times in my streets ministry work, but I have never been blessed with a more loving, caring, compassionate, kind, and caring dispatcher who made clear he wanted me to be with her all the way through until help finally came.

By God's grace, she survived. Police officers arrived. She miraculously perked up and communicated with them. They took over. I left a Gospel tract with her and off I went. I gave the dispatcher my ministry website address with the hope he would visit it and be blessed in so doing.

Now I had a long wait until the next bus came. And after checking online via phone, I knew it would be best to give away my Whole Foods plain chicken and not risk getting sick given how long it would be unrefrigerated and not eaten. God led me to a homeless man whom I am sure enjoyed the chicken.

I am so human. My flesh had wanted to catch that bus. My flesh was tired from an amazing day of ministry. My flesh wanted to get back to my beloved special needs ministry dogs and take care of and be with them. My flesh wanted that chicken. But that lady's survival and hoped for eternity with the Lord was so very much more important.

About two hours after I returned to my hotel, a sister in the Lord who knows me from my a previous stay at the hotel came back from a long day out. She had a whole bunch of grocery bags. She had no idea why but shared with me that God had told her to buy a massive bag of plain rotisserie chicken from Whole Foods. Far, far more than she could possibly eat. Far more than either of us had ever seen a Whole Foods store pack into one carrying case. Two whole chickens it seemed. And she would be delighted if I would accept from her the blessing of a whole bunch of freshly cooked plain chicken from Whole Foods!

I just finished a big bunch of chicken as of the writing of this message. So now I ask you this. Who but God could have orchestrated all this? Who but God so loves His children, so cares about every detail of our lives, and so blesses and honors those who love and serve Him with all our hearts, that all of this would have transpired? Only God! Only the Lord! Praise the Lord!

Hope this little New York City testimony blesses you in reading it as much as it has blessed me being part of it. To the Lord be absolutely every ounce of glory, HALLELUJAH! Amen!

"Every good gift and every perfect gift is from above, and comes down from the Father of lights, with whom there is no variation or shadow of turning." James 1:17 NKJV

"If anyone serves Me, let him follow Me; and where I am, there My servant will be also. If anyone serves Me, him *My* Father will honor." John 12:26 NKJV

...

#98

When We Don't Get Our Way

Per the Bible, God CAN give us exceedingly abundantly more than we can possibly think or imagine, and ALL things are possible to those who believe. But God does NOT promise us He will give us all that we want on this earth! So how do we respond when we don't get our way? Do we respond with love, joy, thanksgiving, and trust in God and in His perfect will and perfect timing for and in our lives? Or, do we act like little children who throw temper tantrums and have pity parties when they don't get all they wish for?

I have spent far too much of my time following Jesus doing the latter like a spoiled child, and I can only imagine how this sin must grieve the heart of our Father in heaven. I am learning to put my trust in God day by day at long last acknowledging that He knows best and to be thankful and rejoice in Him regardless of what He does and doesn't give me when I pray to Him.

And I am learning more and more to pray according to His will instead of according to my own by being filled with and yielded to His Holy Spirit as He directs my prayers in line with the Bible. I am a work in progress, and by God's love, mercy, kindness, and patience, I am growing.

How about you, friend? Do you have some growing to do also in this? Oh, let us grow! Let us repent when we need to repent, and let us place our hearts and trust and very lives in the tender loving merciful hands of the Lord and surrender ourselves wholly with ardent love and joyful thanksgiving to the Lord as He lovingly, patiently, and blessedly conforms us to Himself. Amen!

"Now to Him who is able to do exceedingly abundantly above all that we ask or think, according to the power that works in us, to Him *be* glory in the church by Christ Jesus to all generations, forever and ever. Amen." Ephesians 3:20-21 NKJV

"Jesus said to him, "If you can believe, all things *are* possible to him who believes."" Mark 9:23 NKJV

"Now this is the confidence that we have in Him, that if we ask anything according to His will, He hears us. And if we know that He hears us, whatever we ask, we know that we have the petitions that we have asked of Him." 1 John 5:14-15 NKJV

"Rejoice always, pray without ceasing, in everything give thanks; for this is the will of God in Christ Jesus for you." 1 Thessalonians 5:16-18 NKJV

…

#99

How Can I Possibly REJOICE?

I cannot begin to tell you how many times in recent years the Lord has brought to my attention as I study the Bible the seemingly endless references to being joyful, rejoicing, praising God, celebrating, being happy, making joyful noises, dancing, victory, etc. I used to resent and be jealous of people who were happy because I was so filled with self-pity, sorrow, depression, discouragement, negativity, hurt, bitterness, and the like. The idea that God would call His followers to REJOICE – and to rejoice ALWAYS – was simply beyond my comprehension. But praise God almighty He by His Holy Spirit has given me understanding.

NO MATTER our trials and tribulations, no matter the challenging circumstances of our lives, we can REJOICE IN THE LORD. We can REJOICE THAT ALL WHO TURN FROM OUR SINS, BELIEVE IN HIM AS LORD AND IN HIS DEATH AND RESURRECTION AND TURN TO GOD AND HIS WAYS ARE FORGIVEN AND PROMISED A FOREVER RELATIONSHIP WITH THE LORD AND INDWELT BY HIS HOLY SPIRIT. So it is we who are Jesus' followers can REJOICE IN A FOREVER RELATIONSHIP WITH THE LORD.

We can REJOICE IN KNOWING THAT THOSE OF US WHO BELIEVE IN AND FOLLOW JESUS WILL ONE DAY BE IN GOD'S FOREVER SPLENDOROUS GLORIOUS EVERLASTING PRESENCE.

We can REJOICE IN JESUS. We can REJOICE IN ABIDING IN CHRIST. We can REJOICE IN COMMUNING WITH GOD. We can REJOICE IN HAVING AN INTIMATE RELATIONSHIP WITH GOD. We can REJOICE IN LOOKING FORWARD TO HEAVEN WITH THE LORD. We can REJOICE THAT JESUS IS LORD AND DIED ON THE CROSS FOR US AND WAS RAISED FROM THE DEAD.

We can REJOICE IN GOD'S PROMISES IN THE BIBLE. We can REJOICE THAT GOD BLESSES US EACH AND EVERY DAY. Oh, we can REJOICE IN GOD'S LOVE AND GOODNESS. And on and on the reasons for REJOICING IN THE LORD go. Oh, yes WE CAN – and we SHOULD – REJOICE! Hallelujah!

I am JOYFUL in simply writing this message. Now my encouragement to you – and to myself – is that we CHOOSE to REJOICE ALWAYS – in THE LORD JESUS CHRIST, Hallelujah, PRAISE THE LORD, AMEN!

As we LIVE FOR JESUS, oh, let us REJOICE! To God be the glory – forever! Oh, yes, REJOICE!

"Rejoice in the Lord always. Again I will say, rejoice!" Philippians 4:4 NKJV

"Finally, my brethren, rejoice in the Lord…" Philippians 3:1 NKJV

"For we are the circumcision, who worship God in the Spirit, rejoice in Christ Jesus, and have no confidence in the flesh," Philippians 3:3 NKJV

Maybe you have wondered at times how you can possibly REJOICE given the struggles you face. Let us turn our hearts and faces away from our struggles and set our gazes upon the Lord and REJOICE! Rejoice, rejoice, REJOICE, AMEN!

Rejoicing in Jesus doesn't mean we won't face great challenges. It doesn't mean we'll feel great all the time. It doesn't mean life will be easy.

But at any time of day or night, we can look to the Lord and to His Word and REJOICE! Oh, Hallelujah, oh yes! Amen!

And should our hearts and faces turn away from God and from REJOICING, let us REPENT and turn back to the Lord – AND REJOICE. Hallelujah, Hallelujah, PRAISE THE LORD, AMEN!

…

#100

The Dangers of Devotionals

Years ago, a friend's husband told my friend who relayed to me his belief that God was calling me to write devotionals. I was so prideful at the time that I thought the whole idea ridiculous. First, I decided since the word "devotional" isn't in the Bible that God would not possibly call me to write them. Second, I felt I was being called to write "books" which I suppose in my arrogance I must have figured were more valuable than devotionals. Some years now later, the pride smashed to smithereens, I have written numerous devotional books and countless devotional messages. And I LOVE, LOVE, LOVE writing them. But I am also aware of their dangers and share this warning with you now.

The first danger is we need to NEVER put any book no matter how focused it is on the Lord, no matter how many Bible verses are in it, and no matter how truthful and encouraging the book is above THE LORD and THE BIBLE. Jesus and the Bible and LIVING FOR HIM must come first in our hearts, in our lives, and yes, in our reading!

The second danger is that all humans are fallible, no human writing is perfect, and we need to be enormously careful when we read Christian books including devotionals to measure what we read against the Bible. If we read anything that does not line up with the Bible, that goes against it, we need to let it go. Again, God and the Bible must come first.

So many people use devotionals to help them in their relationship with God and in their alone time with Him. This is all well and wonderful when it is done at the leading of the Holy Spirit, when God is glorified, and when the reader is challenged, encouraged, and helped to grow in faithfully believing in and following and LIVING FOR JESUS. For those who do use devotionals, please do it wisely. Let the Lord lead the way!

And remember number one. The Lord and the Bible. Amen!

A Little Goodbye Letter

Dear Friend,

This isn't a big goodbye. It's just a little one. Sure, this *Live for Jesus* devotional book has come to an end. But it is my hope you might be led to visit my ministry online, to sign up for my free Good News Daily Devotional by email, to reach out to me if the Lord so leads you, and to check out my other books if you are so led. In this case, then this really is just a little goodbye. Either way, thank you for the privilege you have given me of sharing with you these messages the Lord placed on my heart in His call to me to help people become and remain totally devoted followers of the Lord Jesus Christ. In His call to me to help people LIVE FOR JESUS!

With all my heart, I hope you have been blessed and encouraged and inspired and challenged in reading this book. But my heart's cry above all else for you does not concern this book. It is that you will go forth being a totally devoted follower of the Lord Jesus Christ now and forevermore, that you will have a deeply personal, passionate, and intimate relationship with the Lord, that you will be filled with and led by the Holy Spirit of God, that you will be wholly committed to reading and living by the Bible, and that you will seek from God and fulfill His purpose for you personally on this earth!

Friend, please, LIVE FOR JESUS! Hallelujah, AMEN! Praise the Lord!

love, lara

www.GoodNews.love

About Lara Love

I am a 100% Jewish TOTALLY DEVOTED follower of the Lord Jesus Christ once broken for decades beyond human hope & repair and now overflowing with love, hope, peace, joy, passion & purpose on the road for Jesus with my special needs ministry dogs. A writer & evangelist, I write lara love's Good News Daily Devotional online, devotionals, & books; do streets / beach / hotel ministry; create t-shirts & journals; and make Video Devotionals. My life's calling is to be a TOTALLY DEVOTED follower of the Lord Jesus Christ & to help others to become & remain TOTALLY DEVOTED followers of the Lord Jesus Christ. Please visit my ministry online & contact me at:

Lara Love, Good News Ministry
Telephone: 843-338-2219
www.goodnews.love / lara@goodnews.love

♡ Lara Love's **GOOD NEWS DAILY DEVOTIONAL**

LOVE, HOPE, INSPIRATION & ENCOURAGEMENT ♡
delivered by EMAIL almost daily
sign up at **www.GoodNews.love**

Made in the USA
Middletown, DE
09 May 2022

65567420R00106